The Good Funeral Guide

The Good Funeral Guide

Charles Cowling

BLOOMSBURY CONTINUUM
LONDON · OXFORD · NEW YORK · NEW DELHI · SYDNEY

BLOOMSBURY CONTINUUM
Bloomsbury Publishing Plc
50 Bedford Square, London, WC1B 3DP, UK

BLOOMSBURY, BLOOMSBURY CONTINUUM and the Diana logo are trademarks of
Bloomsbury Publishing Plc

First published in Great Britain 2010

A catalogue record for this book is available from the British Library

Library of Congress Cataloguing-in-Publication data has been applied for

ISBN: PB: 978-1-4729-7594-2; eBook: 978-1-4411-1129-6; ePDF: 978-1-4411-3322-9

2 4 6 8 10 9 7 5 3

Designed and typeset by Kenneth Burnley, Wirral, Cheshire

Printed and bound in Great Britain by CPI Group (UK) Ltd, Croydon CR0 4YY

MIX
Paper from
responsible sources
FSC® C013604

To find out more about our authors and books visit www.bloomsbury.com and sign up for our
newsletters

Contents

Acknowledgements

This guide was conceived over lunch with Angie McLachlan, scholar and embalmer, in the George Inn on the Isle of Portland. In due time a draft was born and took its first baby steps on the internet with a note attached to its coat saying, 'Read me and tell me what you think.' The idea at this stage was to link up with like minds, but, though like minds mostly appreciated it, they were also busy with their own projects. Less flatteringly, no plagiarist pirated it.

Now that the guide has reached adulthood, it is time to thank everyone who contributed to its upbringing. I am indebted to Professor Tony Walter and Thomas Lynch for their intellectual guidance and personal indulgence. In the deferential awareness that I am merely a scribbling commentator, I pay tribute to all those thinking, pioneering people who actually make things happen. Many have shared their time and knowledge unstintingly and, with great forbearance, subdued my more boisterous notions and tried to keep me grounded. They are John Mallatrat, Rupert and Claire Callender, James Showers, Ken West, Simon Smith, Jane Morrell, Zinnia Cyclamen, Laura Read, Jonathan Davies, Hazel Warken, Judi Edwards, Nigel Lymn Rose, Ian Gregory, Dave Wheeler, Sheila Dicks, Julie Dunk, Teresa Evans, Kathryn Edwards, Carl Marlow, James Leedam, Rosie Inman-Cook, Susan Morris, Emma Restall-Orr, Tony Piper, Tana Wollen, Anne Barber, Marilyn Watts, friends at Transitus, Cynthia Beal, Holly Stevens, Josh Slocum, Lisa Carlson, Beth Knox, Thomas Friese and Patrick McNally. I am grateful to all those in the funeral industry who have talked to me. Where they have been hospitable, and where they have been hostile, they have always been informative. I thank those who have followed and responded to my blog, where I have been able to try out ideas. The best things in this book are other people's; the errors, only mine.

If, as a society, we don't talk enough about death, no literary agent or publisher can be blamed for concluding that we don't much want to read about it either. I am, therefore, more than ordinarily grateful to my wonderful agent, Jane Graham Maw, for sticking by the manuscript on its long odyssey, to Continuum for offering it landfall, to Caroline Chartres, my editor, for her mind-bracing supervision, and to Kenneth Burnley, who designed this book. I really couldn't have been luckier. Lastly, I offer much more than customary gratitude to Sharon, my wife. The Grim Reaper has been loafing round this house worse than a scowling teenager for too long. It was a lot to ask.

1

What's in this guide?

Read this book if:

- you need to arrange a funeral for someone now;
- you need to find a good funeral director;
- you want to make future arrangements for your own funeral;
- you'd like to learn about death and funerals.

What this guide does

This guide recognizes that you are probably in unfamiliar territory. Most people do not have to arrange more than two funerals in their lifetime.

That's why most people, when they go to a funeral director to make funeral arrangements, do not know what choices are available to them.

Once you have read this guide you will be empowered by knowledge and equipped to take charge.

This guide will inform you speedily and efficiently. It will enable you to:

- take charge of the process of arranging a funeral with confidence;
- find a good funeral director;
- make informed choices about products and services;
- decide what *you* are going to do, and what you are going to pay *others* to do for you;
- get best value for money;
- create a meaningful and memorable funeral ceremony;
- acquire some background information on death and dying, and find out where you can learn more.

Are you web enabled?

This guide does not reproduce information already available on the internet. Instead, it tells you where to find it. Throughout the text you will find signposts to the best websites.

You should read this guide together with the Good Funeral Guide website, which contains additional, up-to-date information on products and services, together with a listing of recommended funeral directors.

* www.goodfuneralguide.co.uk.

If you are reading this guide after someone has died, you will need information about matters like registering the death, what coroners do, probate and other administrative and financial matters.

Get hold of a free copy of the invaluable

* *What To Do After a Death in England or Wales.*

* *What To Do After a Death in Scotland.*

It is published by the Department for Work and Pensions. You can get a copy from a Jobcentre Plus, a social security office, a hospital bereavement office, a registrar, a care home or a local undertaker. You can download a copy at:

* jobcentreplus.gov.uk. Type the title into the search box.

Two other useful books are:

* The *Which* guide *What To Do When Someone Dies.*

* *What To Do Following a Death*, written by Cruse Bereavement Care, published by Lawpack.

Other good books

There are other books about funerals which you may find stimulating and informative. They are:

* *The D-Word* by Sue Brayne (published by Continuum).

* *It's Your Funeral* by Emma George and Roni Jay (published by White Ladder Press Ltd).

* *We Need To Talk About the Funeral* by Jane Morrell and Simon Smith (published by Alphabet & Image Ltd). How to create a memorable funeral ceremony by two experienced practitioners.

* *Time To Go* by Jean Francis (published by iUniverse.com). A survey of over 30 different real-life funerals. A source of great ideas.

What this guide doesn't do

This guide does not reproduce information already widely available on subjects like registering a death, what coroners do, probate and other administrative and financial matters.

This guide does not address the way you are feeling now. We think it cannot be a good idea to offer advice and comfort at the same time. The tone of the guide, therefore, is deliberately matter-of-fact and emotion-free but not, we hope, unsympathetic:

This guide does not deal with ways of coping with grief because there are already plenty of people out there to help you, and lots of literature, and information from

- The BBC: bbc.co.uk/relationships/coping_with_grief/bereavement.
- The Royal College of Psychiatrists: rcpsych.ac.uk – click on 'Mental Health Info'.

A word about words

This guide uses the plain words people normally use. We shall say died, not passed away, body, not remains, and talk about the person who has died, not the deceased. The purpose is not to be insensitive to your feelings but to be straightforward. There is no difference between an undertaker and a funeral director. Most people say undertaker; undertakers wish we would call them funeral directors. This guide uses the terms interchangeably.

2

Take your time

If you are reading this guide because someone is dying or has just died, there seems to be a lot to do.

There is, but it doesn't all have to be done at once.

What is your priority right now?

When someone dies, there is so much to do. Your priorities at this time are to:

- ensure that the body of the person who has died is properly cared for;
- create a fitting funeral ceremony.

Nothing else is more important, however urgent it seems. Until it is over, the funeral comes first. Fit in the other stuff around it.

Right now, you may feel that you urgently need to find a good funeral director.

Alternatively, you may be wondering if you can do the whole thing yourself.

Don't do anything until you have read this guide

There is no point in contacting a funeral director until you know:

- what part, if any, you want to play in caring for the body of the person who has died;
- what goods and services you want to buy from the funeral director;
- what sort of funeral ceremony you want.

This guide will tell you what you need to know. It will put you in the driver's seat.

Read this guide before you act. You have time to do that.

If the death has happened at home there is no urgency to move the person who has died. If, however, an undertaker has already taken the body away, you do not have to make funeral arrangements with that undertaker. So long as you have not signed a contract, you can decide for yourself which funeral home you will use long term, if any, and then have the person who has died brought there.

If the death has happened in a hospital the person who has died can stay in the mortuary for another 24 hours and probably longer.

If the death has happened in a care home or hospice, the authorities will probably want the person who has died moved fast. Hospices have limited facilities for storing bodies, care homes usually none. A care home will want the body moved at once so as not to upset the other residents. If an undertaker has already taken the body away, there's no hurry. So long as you have not signed a contract with that undertaker, you can change your mind and choose someone else – or bring the person who has died home.

If the coroner has ordered a post mortem in order to discover or confirm the cause of death, you will have to wait for the body to be released. There is plenty you can do in the interim.

3

Take charge

You do not have to place yourself in the hands of experts when arranging a funeral.

There is almost nothing you cannot do as well, if not better, yourself.

Who's in charge? See what the law says.

Looking after someone who is dying, then arranging their funeral, can be a disempowering experience. You can find yourself always being sidelined and denied participation by people who know better, first by medical professionals, then, if you're not careful, by the undertaker, and then by the person leading the funeral ceremony.

You can't involve yourself in the work of medical professionals: they are the experts; you have to trust that they know best.

But when someone dies, you can regain a large, even a full measure of control. All you need is enough information to enable you to choose what you want to do. Previous experience is unnecessary and you do not need much expertise – though if you want to do absolutely everything yourself, you will need plenty of practical aptitude.

Most undertakers pride themselves on doing everything for their clients because they think that, considering what they're going through, they won't be up to it. This is the story of most of their clients. It is a temptation to place yourself in the hands of the expert, the undertaker, and say 'Do it all for me.'

No one ever got what they wanted by outsourcing the decision-making to someone who stands to make money out of them.

Clueless clients are very bad for undertakers and no use to themselves. Clients like these make undertakers think they know best, and this is why some of them, beneath their warm and sympathetic smiles, are arrogant or complacent or lazy.

This is because they don't have to try very hard, and the upshot is a 'one size fits all' funeral in which those closest to the person who has died play the part of passive bystanders. This is the story of too many funerals today.

Don't blame the undertakers. They are doing their best, most of them. This is what happens when there are no informed consumers to keep them on their toes and make their lives more interesting.

The more control you take, the harder you'll have to work.

Why would you want to do that?

Because there's every chance that the harder you work at the important things, playing your part in caring for the body of the person who died and creating their funeral ceremony, the better you'll feel. This is a very practical and therapeutic way of expressing and dealing with your sadness.

It will enable you to grieve better at the best time for grieving.

The information contained in this guide will enable you to decide how much you want to do.

Who's in charge?

Who is in charge of arranging the funeral? If this is an issue for you, you need to know what your legal position is.

What's the law?

We have to be blunt. It's the only way you can pin down your legal rights.

The law almost certainly sees things completely differently from you. It concerns itself only with practicalities. It is fuzzy around emotional matters. It doesn't actually care how you feel about what's happened – that's not what the law is for – but it does care what happens next.

You probably want to do two things: first, give the person who has died a good and appropriate funeral; second, either bury or cremate their body. The law is only interested in one thing: getting the body buried or cremated in a legally approved way before it becomes a nuisance to public health.

A funeral is a farewell ceremony or event at which a dead body is present immediately before it is buried or cremated

A funeral fulfils an emotional and sometimes also a spiritual need. You have to understand the precise meanings of words here. Official government guidance uses the term 'funeral arrangements' wrongly to mean disposal arrangements. It may seem kinder to talk about a funeral rather than disposal but it is also, in this respect, misleading. Though we normally think of a funeral as an event comprising a ceremony and either cremation or burial, the law doesn't.

- A funeral is an option, not a legal necessity
- Disposal is compulsory and legally enforceable.

There are three alternatives to immediate disposal, none of which are available to you unless the dead person made provision when they were alive. If the person who has died opted for one of these, you will know all about it. These alternatives are:

- Donation of the body to medical science to be dissected by students. This will delay disposal by up to five years.

- Cryonic preservation: keeping the body frozen in liquid nitrogen until medical science can find a way of reviving it.

- Plastination: a process whereby water is drawn out of the body and replaced by polymers which set hard, after which it is posed and displayed in a Bodyworlds exhibition – see bodyworlds.com.

You do not have to go along with any of them when the time comes.

Who owns a dead body?

In order to facilitate the disposal of the body, the law enables one or more people to take possession of it for that purpose only.

Possession of a dead body is not the same thing as owning it. No one owns a dead body. No one owns a living body, either. You do not own your own body. Are you allowed to offer any of your organs for sale? No, you are not. You do though have rights over what anyone can do to your body – while you're alive.

Certain people have a prior right to possess a dead body so long as they undertake to dispose of it. None of these people has to accept this duty. There is no legal penalty if they refuse, but they won't be able to hold a funeral. If everyone refuses, the dead person's local authority has an inescapable legal duty to dispose of the body (and it will probably hold a funeral, too). It will recoup the expense from the dead person's estate if there are sufficient assets.

The possessor of the body can dispose of it as he or she legally desires, whatever the dead person stipulated when alive.

Those with no automatic rights

There are two categories of people who have no automatic right either to possess the body with the intention of disposing of it or to inherit from the estate.

The first is *next of kin*. The term 'next of kin' is legally meaningless. The person who has died may have nominated someone as his or her next of kin, but that gives them no right to dispose of the body unless named as an executor, and no right to inherit unless named in the will.

The second is an *unmarried partner*, or one who is not legally registered as being in a civil partnership with the person who has died. Such a partner has no right to dispose of the body unless named as an executor, and no right to inherit unless named in the will. This is the cruellest consequence of failing to make a will.

Where there's a will there's an executor

If the person who has died made a will and named an executor, then the executor, whether a family member or not, has the right to possess the body, register the death and make the disposal arrangements, together with the option to arrange a funeral.

But often a person will name more than one executor – for example, his or her children. Who then is the senior executor? The eldest? And what if one of the executors is a local solicitor?

Where there's no will there's an administrator

If the person who has died did not make a will (has died intestate), what then? The answer is that a court of law will appoint the closest living relative to be the administrator of the estate, with inheritance rights and the right to possess the body, register the death and make disposal arrangements, together with the option to arrange a funeral.

If this is your situation, and the court has not yet made a judgement, you can easily predict who the court will nominate. Closest living relatives are sought in strict order: first, a spouse, then children, then parents of the dead person, then brothers and sisters, and so on. Find the full list at the Her Majesty's Courts Service website:

- hmcourts-service.gov.uk. Type 'intestacy rules' into the searchbox.

If there is more than one administrator, who is the senior? The eldest?

The answer is . . .

The answer in both cases is none of them. They are all equal. They are joint possessors of the body. If one of the executors is a local solicitor, he or she is unlikely to meddle unless the family executors start spending too much on the funeral.

Where there is discord

And this, obviously, is where the discord can begin. Where family members have strong and differing views and beliefs, consensus can be hard to come by.

If you are in this position, it is vital that you reach agreement on important matters before one of you registers the death. Each will probably have to give ground over some matters so that each can have his or her way in others. Where victory is impossible, compromise is the sensible outcome.

The buck stops . . .

The person who, at the registrar's office, signs the death certificate will be given a certificate for burial or cremation (the green form) and will be held responsible for making it happen. A registrar will be reluctant to proceed with registration if it is evident that the executors are wrangling.

The person who makes arrangements with a funeral director makes him- or herself responsible for paying the bill. A funeral director will be reluctant to enter into a contract if he or she is aware of strife. Having done so, the funeral director will answer directly to the contractee and no one else.

When you register the death

Don't rush down to the registrar to register the death. Take as long as you need to get together all the documents and information you need. If you give any wrong information it will have to be changed. This will cost time, hassle and, possibly, money.

You need to register the death within five days.

If the death has been reported to the coroner, there may or may not be an inquest. Whichever, the coroner will send necessary paperwork to the registrar who will register the death and inform you.

You can't make final arrangements for the disposal of the body – and, therefore, arrange a funeral – until you have got that green form. You can, though, make provisional arrangements.

If you opt for cremation, the application form will ask you: 'Is there any near relative(s) or executor(s) who has not been informed of the proposed cremation?' This is to prevent someone from cremating the body without your knowledge, and to prevent you from cremating it without your fellow executors' or administrators' knowledge. It also covers a circumstance where an executor refuses to arrange disposal and someone else undertakes to do so instead.

The form will also ask you: 'Has any near relative or executor expressed any objection to the proposed cremation?' This is to prevent a funeral from taking place to which an executor objects. A dissenting executor has a legal right to take out an injunction to this effect.

Are you sure you want to have a funeral? Chapter 5 will help you make your mind up.

Who can you give your body to?

Until recently this legal concept prevailed: 'The only lawful possessor of the dead body is the earth.' The concept derives from church law, which says that a body belongs to God, and also perhaps from Roman law which said that only a slave can be owned. So: you can't own yourself, neither can anyone else.

When a death is registered, the local authority is alerted so that it can make sure the body is buried or cremated under the terms of the Public Health (Control of Disease) Act 1984.

But a recent court case overturned this. It concerned a tramp called Diogenes and his friend the painter Robert Lenkiewicz. As he lay dying in 1984, Diogenes bequeathed his body to the painter. Lenkiewicz accepted the gift and embalmed the dead Diogenes. Before long, Plymouth City Council officials came looking for the body, determined to dispose of it themselves if the artist wouldn't. Lenkiewicz hid Diogenes and refused to tell them where he was. Years passed. Lenkiewicz died and Diogenes was discovered in a drawer. The council returned and more angry wrangling ensued until in 2002 the coroner ruled that, because the body had been embalmed, Lenkiewicz and then his estate had the right to continued possession of it for as long as the embalmed Diogenes complies with laws governing environmental health and public decency.

If you want to donate your body to anyone, its new owner will have to do the same.

4

Take stock

Here are some things you and your family need to start thinking about, talking about and taking into consideration – because every family does things its own way.

Note: you do not have to reach immediate decisions.

The aftermath of every death is unique. There is the emotional impact. There are all the things that need to be done. People always say how busy they are.

If you are reading this just after someone has died, you will find that being effective when you are grieving isn't easy. Even when you feel you are doing well, you are probably not coping as well as you think you are. Perhaps it's only when you look back that you'll be able to see this.

Purposeful activity may be useful therapy. It may also be ineffectual displacement activity and no less valuable. Washing china ornaments at two in the morning may be exactly what you need to be doing.

If you are an active member of a faith community, and the person who has died was, too, there are probably established duties and rituals laid down for you – a prescribed way of doing things plus a support network of leaders and members. These rituals will make things more straightforward and their familiarity will doubtless bring you comfort.

If you are a member of the secular majority you have many choices to make and you will probably have to start more or less from scratch.

Make lists

You'll need to keep an eye on the value of what you're doing or you're going to miss something important. There are things that need doing now, things that can wait a little and things that can wait longer. So it'll probably be worth your while to:

- take a large sheet of paper;
- rule three vertical columns;
- give them headings like Short Term, Medium Term, Long Term;
- keep it where everyone can add to it.

Write things down as you think of them. Agree priorities – continuously. Column one may need to be re-ordered often, probably on a separate sheet of paper.

Start jotting.

Timescales

If you opt for burial, you ought to be able to hold the funeral within a few days. If you opt for cremation, it could be a fortnight or even longer. The paperwork can take a long time to come through. It can be difficult, especially at busy times of the year, to book the day and, especially, the time you want.

Very few crematoria operate at what you might reckon to be the best time for funeral. Some hold funerals at weekends, none in the evenings. The same goes for local authority-owned cemeteries, should you opt for burial. An exception is made for Muslims on religious grounds, an arrangement which does not require local authority staff to work overtime because Muslims use pre-prepared graves.

So the sooner you can book your slot, the sooner you will be able devise a timeframe for everything else.

Telling people

You are going to need to start telling people what has happened. Start with the bank. In addition to all the people you can think of, there will be those in the address book of the person who has died. There may also be friends and neighbours unknown to you who are not listed.

Here's a job you may like to share out.

In order to make sure you reach everybody, put an announcement in your local paper when you know when the funeral is going to be.

If you think that might expose you to burglary when the funeral is happening, contact your local neighbourhood policing team for advice and support.

- Get the phone number from the Directgov website.

Things to ponder

This guide will help you to prioritize – to assess the value and urgency of what needs to be done. But even as you are listing things that need to be done now, it's worth mulling over matters that only you can evaluate over the coming days. Here are some.

How does everyone feel?

For those left behind, death generates an emotional overload. Immediately after a death, emotions can be very raw and people can behave irrationally and unpredictably without knowing it. You too, perhaps.

This can lead to communication difficulties.

What are these raw emotions?

Every death generates different emotions in different people, of differing intensity. These emotions may include shock, disbelief, desolate sadness, panic, anger and guilt, at times singly, and sometimes all mixed up together. They may produce physical symptoms.

Sometimes they generate hysterical giggles.

Children are a special case (see below).

Dominant emotional responses will depend on who has died and in what circumstances. The death of an old person after a long period of frailty may bring with it a sense of relief. The death of a young person or someone who has committed suicide may generate great anger. The death of a baby may make the parents feel guilty that they got something wrong. All the other grief emotions are likely to be present, too.

Of all these emotions the most irrational-seeming and difficult to deal with in yourself and others is blitz-strength anger. Often, people lash out at others and accuse them and blame them completely unreasonably and unfairly. If this happens with a member of your family, bite your tongue and wait for the storm to pass.

The emotion which is hardest for people to deal with is guilt.

Shock

What does shock feel like? It feels like this. You see the world going on around you. You are hyper-conscious of it. You can't believe that people – strangers – would just carry on as normal after what has happened. You may, perhaps, think you occasionally hear the person who has died. When you are out, you think you glimpse them in a crowd.

That's shock.

Don't force the pace

If you, together with other members of your family, are going to plan the funeral together, bear in mind that, even if you mostly agree, reasoned discussion may, at times, break down under the weight of shock and emotion. You may even find yourself going off on one from time to time. Quite possibly no one will behave very well all the time. That's normal.

Another good reason for giving it time. Don't force the pace. Wait for people's minds to make themselves up.

Who gets what?

If the contents of the house are going to be divided up, and you can find no instructions about who is to have precisely what, there could be tense discussions leading to acrimonious rows.

This may be inevitable. Try, though, to defuse things by postponing decision-making for as long as possible in the hope that sense will finally break through the fog of emotion. Insist that this can wait till after the funeral. It can.

How much time do you need to take off work?

Most workplaces are reluctant to give employees more than a few days off work when someone dies. This is arguably foolish. An emotionally healthy employee is more valuable than an emotionally distracted one.

You need to ask yourself which is more important: the dead or the living? What you need to do at work or what you need to do at home?

Where are you going to be of most use? Where ought you to be?

Your employer may be displeased to learn how much time you reckon you need. A clear sense of duty will help you to stick to your guns.

Family matters

A funeral is usually a family affair – one of those occasions, like weddings, when everyone comes together. In most families there are tensions between some members; rifts, possibly; even feuds. There could be tactful times ahead.

Who could be difficult? Ask yourself this: how does your family handle weddings?

Previous partners

And here's another thing: did the person who has died have any previous partner or partners? Or a lover? What role, if any, do you want them to play in the funeral? This may be an agonizingly difficult matter to resolve, especially if you have half-brothers or half-sisters.

A funeral can easily be blown apart by the unexpected arrival and even the uninvited participation of a ghost from the past – or the present.

Children

Children are affected by death differently from adults. Depending on how old they are, they will ask you questions which you will need to be able to answer. There is general agreement that truth is better than euphemisms. Use the d-word and don't give them lots of airy-fairy stuff about going to a better place. Read more in Chapter 18.

Find good advice online here:

* hospicenet.org. Go to Services, then to Caregivers.

* winstonswish.org.uk. Go to Parents/Carers.

Some good storybooks which explain death to children are:

* *Badger's Parting Gifts* by Susan Varley, published by HarperCollins. Shows how people who have died leave living memories to those left behind.

* *Grandad's Ashes* by Walter Smith, published by Jessica Kingsley. Brilliant story about the problem of finding the right time and place to scatter ashes.

* *When Someone Very Special Dies* by Marge Heegard, published by Woodland Press. Lots of drawing exercises which enable children between six and twelve to work out their feelings.

Friends and neighbours

While you are struggling to come to terms with how you feel, you may find that some of your friends and neighbours are struggling, too – with how to talk to you about what has happened. Bereaved people sometimes feel as if they are a social embarrassment, especially when they see a neighbour furtively cross the street to avoid them.

In a society which doesn't talk enough about death, and in which much of the vocabulary of everyday courtesy has been lost, there are few words for the bereaved. People think there's nothing they can do to help. They fear you will never stop talking or, worse, break down. So they go schtum. Be prepared.

Those who ask 'Is there anything I can do?' almost certainly mean it. Helping you will make them feel useful and no longer powerless. You've got a list. Give them things to do. You'll be doing them – and yourself – a favour.

How should you behave?

When death happens in a movie, there is customarily a sequence where, accompanied by plaintive string music, the hero, suspended in grief, beggared by misery, walks aimlessly along rainswept streets, sits huddled, stares into the distance – that sort of thing. This single mood may seem to be model behaviour. It may be how other people expect bereaved people to behave and how you think you ought to behave all the time.

But in real life people carry on – because life goes on. So there's no single right way to behave, no emotional best practice. Try not to be self-conscious. If you find yourself laughing at something on the television, that's okay.

You've got enough on your emotional plate without playing a part or worrying about what anyone else thinks.

Doing what's expected

If you want to have a funeral ceremony, you probably want to do what is expected of you, especially by the person who has died.

How much *do* you know about what the person who died wanted?

If you don't know much, you should think twice about imposing your own values and beliefs on the funeral ceremony. If, for example, the person who has died was not religious, but you are, a religious ceremony will probably miss the point.

The funeral is for the person who died.

Start sorting out the paperwork

Have a sift through the paperwork of the person who's died. If you don't know what they wanted, you may find something that tells you.

Sorting through this paper will also give you a rough idea of other things that need to be done. Most of them can wait.

Is there a funeral plan?

Is there a pre-need funeral plan which will pay for the funeral? If you are not sure, have a look for one. It may have one of these titles: Golden Leaves, Golden Charter, Dignity Funeral Plan, Age Concern Funeral Plan. The important words to look for are Funeral Plan.

Undertakers love funeral plans. They sell as many as they can. This tells you who does better out of them.

A funeral plan can be a great relief for people who are newly bereaved. It saves a lot of hassle and decision-making because it takes care of almost all that. It covers most of the costs and it lays down exactly what the person who has died wanted. It specifies, for example, type of coffin and the number of vehicles to follow the hearse. After a short chat with the funeral director, you will have little else to do except wait for the day.

The downside is that the plan may tie you into a funeral director you find you dislike. Some plans will allow you to change funeral director, and every plan will allow you to buy more expensive services. But what if you can't find what you want? What if you decide to do it all yourself and have a home-arranged funeral?

If you don't like the funeral plan, can you get the money back? Yes, you can. But you won't get the matured sum, only what it cost – less an administration fee of around £155.

Impossible final requests

If the person who has died was especially well prepared and brave, he or she may have made funeral plans which they did not discuss with you and which you find you do not like.

For instance, they may have left detailed instructions with a celebrant or event organizer. They may have included instructions in a pre-paid funeral plan. They may have recorded a hilarious DVD to be played at the funeral which, in your sadness, you feel will be unbearable. They may have chosen music which you consider to be out of place. They may have left strict instructions that no one is to attend the funeral, not even those closest to them.

Are you obliged to go along with any of this?

No, not if you feel strongly enough. Dead people have limited rights in deciding the content of their funeral, and none at all in regulating the emotions of those left behind. Death is a very good time to let go.

The funeral is for you, too.

Other people

If you want to have an open-invitation funeral, you need to start thinking about what those who will want to come are likely to expect, and then decide to what extent you are going to do what they want. If, for example, you decide you want a non-religious funeral, what about those relatives and friends who are religious? If you want a full-on religious funeral, what about all those unbelievers and don't-knows who may feel alienated and for whom the ceremony may lack any relevance? Is there a compromise? If you want everyone to wear bright clothes, what about the feelings of those people who will be expecting something more formal and, as they might put it, respectful?

The funeral is for them, as well.

There is no need to make snap decisions.

Do you want a funeral at all?

Everyone will expect you to hold a funeral, but it may be that you feel that a funeral is a pointless, meaningless exercise. What is the point in just going through the motions? Do you actually want to have a funeral at all? Why do we have funerals?

The next chapter will help you think this through.

5

Why do we have funerals?

What is a funeral for?

Is it really necessary to have the body at the funeral?

If you can see no point in holding a funeral . . .

What the law says.

> I'm dreading the funeral – absolutely dreading it. I was with him when he died. I know he's gone. As far as I'm concerned it's all over. So what on earth is the point of going through it all again? It's morbid and horrible.

If you are an active member of a faith group which believes that a funeral ritual is desirable or necessary to enable the spirit of the person who has died to pass across into eternity, you know exactly what a funeral is for and you do not need to read this chapter.

If you have no strong faith, you may wonder whether a funeral is really necessary. You have possibly been to more than one bleak, meaningless funeral which missed the point at every turn. Funerals in this country over the last 40 years have often been dire.

If you are an atheist, you may have strong ideas about the status of the body after death.

Read on, take a fresh look and make up your mind for yourself.

There's no point in holding a funeral if you don't know exactly why you're doing it. So: why do we have funerals?

Because death is not the end

We have funerals because death is not the end.

It takes the life of the one you love . . . and leaves behind a body which must be disposed of by burial or cremation, a physical task requiring a practical arrangement.

Death also takes people close to us whom we may not love – an abusive parent or partner.

Every culture from earliest times has cared for its dead and created its own funeral ceremonies and rituals. They have no practical value. They mark the significance and the magnitude of the passing of a life.

One way of looking at it is to say that how we value our dead says a lot about how we value the living. That is why, traditionally, important people have been given very elaborate funerals and the worst criminals none at all.

There's an opposite way of looking at it. When the playwright Arthur Miller was asked if he'd be going to the funeral of his ex-wife, Marilyn Monroe, he replied, 'Why should I go? She won't be there.' A funeral is pointless, he reckoned, both for the dead and for the living. It's not the body that's important, but the person whom it embodied – the vitality which animated it. When death comes, that's it.

You can dispose of a body in a ceremonial way by holding a funeral, or you can arrange to have it buried or cremated with no one there. The consequence for the body is the same in either case.

What is a funeral for?

If it makes no difference to a body if it gets a funeral or not, what is a funeral for? Consider the following statements. Do they say what you think? Take a pencil and tick the statements you agree with.

- ☐ Letting go of someone's body with love and care is the last thing you can do for them in this world.
- ☐ A funeral is a precious gift to the person who has died.
- ☐ A funeral is for all those people, family, friends and neighbours, who were not present at the death. It is their time to pay their respects and say goodbye.
- ☐ It is a time to express sorrow.
- ☐ It is a time when people can comfort each other.
- ☐ It is a time to take stock of what the person who has died means to you and others and, more important, will go on meaning.
- ☐ It is a time to say thank you to the person who has died.

If you agree with most or all of these statements, then you will probably be persuaded of the value of holding a funeral.

Is it really necessary to have the body at the funeral?

It has always been the custom to hold a funeral with the body present because the funeral is an integral part of the process of disposal. And yet you can accomplish most of the things listed above without a body present. What difference would that make?

Given our feelings about dead bodies, nothing concentrates the mind like being in the same room as one. When that dead body is someone you know, it brings home the reality of the death and greatly enhances the drama of the occasion.

Perhaps you feel that a funeral with a body is unnecessarily upsetting, morbid, even, especially if the person who has died was young. In that case you could organize a small funeral for close family and friends and then follow it with a celebration-of-life party at a venue of your choice to which everyone else is invited to eat, drink, listen to music and share happy memories.

A drawback here may be that those not invited to the funeral will feel that they can't enter fully into the jollity of the life celebration because they never got a chance to express their grief and say goodbye first. They may even feel cheated or patronized. It can be hard to do the fun bit if you haven't done the sad bit first. If people are hurting, you probably need to address those feelings before moving them on to happy memories. A death is exactly as sad as it is, and there is nothing you can say or do to make it otherwise.

So a funeral without a body may feel like a diluted event. It may lack focus and substance and reality. It may lack power. A baby-naming or christening wouldn't be the same without a baby, and a wedding or civil partnership ceremony wouldn't be the same without the happy couple. If that logic extends to funerals, you need a body.

What is a dead body?

Much depends on what you reckon will be the status of your body when you're dead. Here are three ways of looking at it. Which is your way? What were the views of the person who has died?

☐   My body and my soul belong together (I am not dead, I am sleeping).

☐   I had a body. Now I am a spirit (my body is old clothes).

☐   I had a body. Now I am no more (ditto).

When you are alive, who you are is very much tied up with what you look like. Your body is the embodiment of all that you are, an essential component of your identity. By your body, others know you. It is you made manifest. And just as your body is precious to you, so are the bodies of those you love.

Death makes all the difference. A person's personality is very evidently absent from their dead body. Their dead body is clearly not them any more. 'It's only a shell', people say (for all that a dead body is nothing like a shell).

Which causes us to wonder, some of us, about the soul, the spirit, where that's gone, if anywhere, and what is the relationship between body and spirit – are they one or are they separate? Do we get to be resurrected in our earthly body? Does our spirit live on in some other way?

If you believe that the spirit survives death, and that's what you want to focus on, you may consider the dead body to be an irrelevance and a distraction.

When John Lennon was killed, Yoko Ono wanted no focus on his bullet-ridden corpse. She had it cremated unceremoniously, unwitnessed. She held a memorial ceremony instead, to take place everywhere and anywhere. 'Pray for his soul from wherever you are', she said. And people did. Presumably this is what John wanted, too.

By contrast, Michael Jackson's body was held precious and was present at his memorial concert encased in a bronze, gold-plated, $25,000 Batesville casket.

If you are arranging a funeral for someone, you will probably reckon it important to accord at least as much status to their body as they did – possibly more.

Direct cremation

If you decide as Yoko Ono did, you too can opt for *direct cremation*: arrange for the body to be taken straight from the place of death and cremated without a funeral. There is presently just one direct cremation specialist in the UK, Simplicity Cremations:

- simplicitycremations.co.uk.

Direct cremation as a preparation of the body for a funeral

Direct cremation may also be seen as a way of preparing a body for a funeral and disposal. It renders it portable, stable, durable and divisible.

So, instead of holding a funeral for the body, you can hold one for the ashes. If you'd like to hold a funeral or a commemorative event in a place dear to the person who has died, you can do that much more easily and cheaply with ashes than with a dead body.

A memorial service

A funeral without a body is what we customarily call a *memorial service*. A memorial service takes place some time after a funeral and is especially convenient for people who can't find time at short notice to make it to the real thing. Now that many people live far away from where they were born and brought up, memorial services are becoming more popular. You can give people lots of notice. And if you opted for cremation, you can have the ashes there too, if you like.

What's new about funerals today?

Until around fifteen years ago nothing much changed in the world of death. Almost every funeral, under the influence of the Protestant death ethic, was brief, simple and bleak, every one the same.

Throughout the last fifteen years, as society has become more openly secular and individualistic, people have begun to demand funerals which express a different spirit and a different spirituality – or none at all.

The baby-boomers have played their part. When they were young they reinvented youth culture. As they approach their dotage they are reinventing death culture. They are reclaiming funerals from strangers – the priests and the undertakers – and they are refashioning funeral rituals for their dead. They say that death is a taboo in our society, and that's become a cliché because it is repeated by the media every time they talk about it, which is all the time. We are a death-aware society, looking for better ways to die and better ways to send off our dead. Look how many people know exactly which song they want to be played at their funeral.

These are the features of an increasing number of present-day funerals:

*   *Secular or spiritual* – rejecting orthodox religious rituals.

*   *Personalized* – a funeral as unique as the life lived which focuses on the person who has died and celebrates their life.

*   *Participative* – the engagement of family and friends in caring for the body of the dead person and creating their farewell ceremony.

*   *Iconoclastic* – preferring gratitude to gloom, laughter to lamentation and wacky music choices – 'Another One Bites the Dust'; 'Bat Out of Hell', 'Always Look on the Bright Side of Life'.

6

What is a green funeral?

Is it for you?

How green do you want it?

Find a natural burial ground.

A green funeral seeks, if not to enrich the environment, then at least not to harm it. It is an ethical choice.

Environmentalism is a secular hellfire religion which encompasses cults, sects, denominations, prophets, gurus, apostates, zealots, lipservers, charlatans and heretics for whom, whatever their points of disagreement, a green funeral is a contemporary, forward-looking response to urgent ecological challenges, particularly climate change. There are environmentalists who are climate-change deniers and environmentalists who believe that no amount of carbon sequestration will make a blind bit of difference. To all of these, too, a green funeral may make ethical sense.

Like all progressive movements in the world of funerals, a green funeral reinvents the past. The essence of a green funeral is age-old elemental simplicity, which many reckon also to be beautiful. So a green funeral is an aesthetic choice, too, and for this reason may appeal also to people with no interest in environmental issues whatsoever. It rejects the so-called traditional funeral with its stuffy, Victorian, urban look, in favour of an outdoors, homespun, back-to-nature look. It prefers an unspoilt landscape to that of a regimented conventional cemetery. If it's a look you like, natural burial is as lovely as it gets.

But ethics and aesthetics are not always reconcilable, as we shall see.

What's the appeal for you – the ethics or the aesthetic? Both? Read and decide.

An extreme green funeral

Here are the elements of a real green funeral:

- Rejects cremation.
- Opts for burial in a site serving a conservation purpose.
- Creates an environment which is not visually definable as a burial ground.
- Reviles embalming.

- Requires a coffin or shroud locally made from natural, sustainable materials.

- Prefers a hand-dug grave.

- Buries the body at a depth where it can decompose aerobically.

- Rejects bought flowers, favours garden flowers (if any).

- Forbids demarcation of the grave.

- Forbids marking or personalizing of the grave with any sort of permanent memorial.

- Forbids tending of the grave.

- Discourages visits to the grave unless on foot or bike.

A real green funeral leaves no trace behind,

> Annihilating all that's made,
> To a green thought in a green shade. (Andrew Marvell)

It inhabits the spirit of Psalm 103: 'As for man, his days are as grass: as a flower of the field, so he flourisheth. For the wind passeth over it, and it is gone; and the place thereof shall know it no more.'

It is not the grave that commemorates the life lived, it is the entire site

There are presently very few, if any, natural burial grounds which meet all the above criteria – nor clients prepared to meet them, either.

Down to earth

Most people who favour natural burial want their decomposed body to be useful to the soil and the plants that grow in it. Natural burial is a very personal form of recycling. Many like the idea of having a tree planted on top of them.

But a dead body will nourish the environment best if it can decompose aerobically. This means burying it in the layer of the soil where bugs and microbes abound, normally the top two feet.

In a local authority cemetery, by law, no part of a coffin must be less than three feet below the surface except where soil conditions allow, in which case two feet will do, too deep to ensure really vibrant aerobic decomposition. This law does not apply to private burial grounds, but the Ministry of Justice is urging compliance.

Almost all natural burial grounds bury bodies at a depth where decomposition will be cold, slow and mostly anaerobic. Are they practising a deception when, in their publicity materials, they encourage the fond belief that the bodies they bury will soon be part of the cycle of nature? Why do they do it?

First, they claim that a shallow burial will render the body prey to badgers and foxes. There is no evidence to back their misgivings. Foxes are idle opportunists; badgers prefer snails and slugs. In the face of persisting anxiety, the simple enough solution is to put fencing wire a few inches below the soil on top of the grave. That would deter any marauding creature.

Second, natural burial grounds worry about smells emanating from shallow graves. But there are no studies that show whether this would be a problem, and if so, how much. Thus can soft aesthetics crowd out tough ethics.

Here's another way of looking at it, from Emma Restall Orr of Sun Rising natural burial ground, near Banbury: 'The idea is poetic, not practical, and we make this clear to any families who enquire. Though sentimental images are valuable in the process of grieving and healing, the ethos of a natural burial ground is (for us) real, down to earth, practical care for the deceased, their families, and the environment, not poetry. First of all, most native trees don't require rich soil, many preferring soil that is not well fertilized. Secondly, burial returns the body's elements back into the cycles of nature, long term – in a way that cremation does not. The planting of the tree adds to the health of those cycles, and the richness of the environment generally. And this is enough.'

Do natural burial grounds recycle?

When a natural burial ground is created out of farmland, it does not necessarily take that land out of agricultural cultivation. In some, use is limited either to timber production or grazing. Others are managed as wildlife habitats.

Some natural burial grounds are zones in conventional local authority cemeteries which have been set aside for natural burial.

None has a policy for recycling land, where feasible, and operating a re-use of graves policy. This would enhance sustainability and bring down burial costs.

Once a body is skeletized, in around ten years, it is arguably time to move on, make room and re-use the grave. In the Middle Ages they had charnel houses to put dug-up bones in, but these seem unlikely to make a comeback. An alternative would be to dig up the bones, grind them and scatter them over the woodland or meadow – or give them to next-of-kin. Aesthetically this is a disaster of a proposal, yet that's exactly what we do to bones of bodies burnt in a crematorium. It is legally objectionable, too: you'd need an exhumation order to do it. But let's get real, it makes good green sense, doesn't it? Or does it? Some green buriers argue for this (most don't). The Government shirks the issue at every turn.

What shade of green are you?

Natural burial grounds have some way to go to become truly green, a truly ethical option for deep greens, and they shrink from becoming so because they are commercial operations which need to be alluring to consumers. They can only move at the pace of public attitudes.

How much greener is a green funeral than a conventional funeral?

It's the living, not the dead, who are costing us the earth. A conventional funeral is not eco-hostile when you compare it with the environmental price of keeping someone alive, feeding them, clothing them, warming them, transporting them, taking them on holiday and keeping them supplied with consumer goods. This being the case, a typical green funeral might be viewed by greener-than-thou fundamentalists as an act of atonement for a life which consumed far too much energy – and a gestural act at that. Only if the person who has died had made every effort to minimize their impact when they were alive does a green funeral make sequential sense.

In the great scheme of things, a green funeral still isn't, in itself, actually going to make much difference or put anything right. It only takes one person to fly in for it to blot out the benefit. But it is emblematic. It sets a good example. It is a step in the right direction.

Conventional burial is not in itself environmentally costly. It's the price of maintaining the cemetery over the years by people with machines that racks up the damage – all that mowing. This is why many local authorities have allocated sections of their cemeteries to natural burial and permitted them to become wildlife habitats. It makes good environmental sense. At the same time, lower maintenance costs in terms of manpower and machinery make excellent financial sense to council taxpayers.

A rural natural burial ground can be just as environmentally damaging as a conventionally managed, manicured local authority cemetery. How so? Because if you can't get to it by bus, regular visits by car will soon rack up a sizeable carbon exhaust-cloud.

To cremate a body consumes roughly as much energy as that person would have consumed domestically in a month – for most, a tiny fraction of the energy they consumed in a lifetime. But the environmental cost, and it's a high one, comes with the emissions. The vapourized mercury from dental amalgam can now be captured – but has to be disposed of in landfill. Dioxins escape, and they are carcinogenic.

Losing the plot

Most natural burial grounds will not let you delineate the grave, tend it nor mark it with a permanent memorial – a headstone. It is simply not in the spirit of natural burial. The position of the grave is recorded (it's a legal requirement), and you will be able to find it by GPS, by microchip buried in the grave or with a tape measure.

Remember: it is the entire place and its surroundings that stand as a memorial to each dead resident.

Some burial grounds will let you mark the grave with a temporary marker, usually a wooden one. Others will let you mark the grave with a small, simply worded stone marker laid flat. Some will allow nothing at all.

If you are considering natural burial, you need to think hard about this. It is a deep-seated spiritual and psychological need in many people to memorialize the life by marking the spot.

Eco-puritans characterize this as vanity. Instead, they say, of showing how much you care about your dead person by tending their grave, why don't you demonstrate that care by allowing nature to receive them back and enable them to create habitats?

For all that, and without going deeply into reasons why, it is observable that many people need material and personalized symbols to identify with, and they need them very much. For them, a natural burial ground may be indistinguishable from a mass grave. They need to be able to see a sign.

Those natural burial grounds which permit a certain amount of gardening of the grave find it impossible to hold the line. Graves start to get cluttered with all sorts of memorial items: plaster figures, wind chimes, teddy bears, artificial flowers and all the paraphernalia you expect in a conventional cemetery. You find bedecked graves next to unkempt graves – graves as nature intended. The burial ground begins to look like a shanty town of the dead.

Attempts to stem this tide of what natural burial guru Ken West terms 'grieving waste' whip up strong emotion. Civil war breaks out among grave visitors. It is a civil war between two utterly opposed and irreconcilable mindsets, and it is waged in conventional cemeteries, too. There is sometimes an element of aesthetic snobbery involved. Which side are you on?

Some people choose natural burial primarily for ethical reasons. Others are refugees from conventional cemeteries, which they reckon to be eyesores. Both groups deplore 'grieving waste' either because they think it spoils the natural look of the burial ground or because they think it denotes vanity or because they think it is, snobbishly you might say, repellently naff – visual jabber.

Some people who choose natural burial find not being able to mark and tend the grave hard to bear. If the burial ground is remote, they can't get around to visiting as often as they'd like.

There are other ways to commemorate someone. Read Chapter 41.

Why is there no rating system?

Natural burial grounds vary greatly in terms of environmental goals, appearance and ambience. The only way to find the right one for you is to go and look.

Why is there no green rating or certification scheme? Would this be useful?

Possibly not, and for these reasons:

- Natural burial is still very new. The first ground was created at Carlisle in 1993. There are now more than 200, the number is growing and the way they do things still evolving.

- Rating systems encourage standardization, discourage variety and can serve as a guise for marketing. Green comes in many shades, and talk of greenwashing at this stage is probably unfair.

- Not enough science has been done yet. We don't yet know enough to enable us to define or agree, best ecological strategies, let alone goals.

- Ratings and certification are objective. But people's experience of a natural burial ground is subjective, also, and incapable of evaluation. For this reason, Cemetery of the Year awards miss the point. It's all too much a matter of taste.

- People's experience of a natural burial ground as a place of ceremonial, commemoration and communion with the dead goes well beyond its greenness or its aesthetic appeal, and is highly personal. Certification couldn't embrace this.

Green products

You can green your funeral with one of a variety of ethically sourced coffins which are just as attractive to people who simply like the look of them. You may prefer a lovely leaf shroud from Bellacouche (see Chapter 39).

If you like to source your goods locally, and entertain intuitive misgivings about willow coffins from Poland or bamboo from China, you may be relieved to find that their carbon footprint is often no greater.

Find out more about coffins in Chapter 39.

Fad or trad?

Is natural burial a passing fashion or is it here to stay? It is hard to predict. There have always been those who favour simple funerals and those who favour elaborate funerals, and there has often been a prevailing convention for one or the other. For environmental and aesthetic reasons, natural burial would seem to be both durable and capable of adapting to new methods of disposal like resomation and cryomation (see Chapter 8).

But a natural burial ground is not a memorial landscape. It does not speak of those buried in it, and for this reason it may fail to satisfy the emotional and spiritual needs of those left behind, for whom environmentalism is not enough.

Victorian cemeteries and their successors failed because, filled as they are with individual memorials which speak of those buried in them, they don't pay their way financially or ecologically. They impose intolerable burdens of funding and maintenance on succeeding generations. In their various stages of neglect they are green spaces which harbour all manner of wildlife and some high quality memorial art. For all that, their report card reads 'Could do better'. Natural burial is a reaction against them. It might be argued that it is an overreaction.

For this reason there will doubtless be those in the future who seek to create memorial landscapes which integrate and serve environmental, spiritual and commemorative needs, and establish a symbiotic partnership between humankind and nature.

Value for money

The cost of a grave in a natural burial ground normally starts at around £500 and can rise to £7,000 depending on the beauty of the location and the position of the plot. Natural burial grounds do not benefit, as do local authorities, from tax breaks and subsidies from cremation, yet they are competitively priced. What's more, you save yourself the cost of a headstone.

Whether or not some of them are fiscally sound has been questioned. Seek assurances.

Some are idealistic enterprises set up by charities, many are set up by farmers, and a few are simply in it for as much money as they can make.

Many allow you to bury or scatter ashes. Some will bury an embalmed body. What environmental sense does that make, you may ask.

Many do not have a building in which you can hold a funeral ceremony. While a tent of some sort erected by the grave may keep off the worst of the weather, a natural burial ground on a rainy day in February is not the sort of place you want to hang around in.

Find out more

- The Association of Natural Burial Grounds lists all green grounds in the UK: http://www.anbg.co.uk/.

- Assess the environmental impact of your funeral: http://www.iccm-uk.com/downloads/Ken.pdf.

Tree of life

It's one thing to have a tree planted on your grave, but what happens if the tree is blown over in a gale? You could be held aloft in the embrace of its roots, your grinning skeleton exposed for all to see.

An alternative is to *become* that tree, and scientific artists Georg Tremmel and Shiho Fukuhara have shown us how. They have found a way of combining human DNA with the DNA of a tree without genetically modifying the tree. You don't need to be under the tree; you don't even need to be dead. They call these trees Transgenic Tombstones. All they need is a swab from the inside of your mouth and you can become, say, an apple tree and live on long after you have conked out. Difficult to know how your nearest and dearest might feel about eating your apples, though. Cost: around £20,000. Find out more at biopresence.com.

7

Burial or cremation?

Earth or fire?

Is there no other way?

Which is cheaper?

Which is greener?

Back in the dawn of time, thousands of years ago, people disposed of their dead in one of two ways. Fast-forward to the present, you find that time has stood still. Your principal choices remain, now as then: burial or cremation.

It's an elemental business, death. Earth and fire are its elements. Disposal methods are eternal: earthly bodies go back to the earth one way or another.

It's not over till it's over

By now you have probably begun to sort out your ideas about the purpose and value of a funeral ceremony and you understand that you can go about that in a number of ways or none at all.

In the matter of disposing of the body, however, you have no choice at all. One way or the other, it's got to go.

If the person who has died made his or her wishes known, you probably want to do what they want. However, even if they did express a preference, and even left strict instructions, it's still your decision. You can overrule their instructions. So, if you want to be sure that *your* executors do as *you* ask, your best bet is to make that a condition of your will – they don't get to inherit unless they do what you say.

Some religions do not allow you the choice. But in case you need to make a decision, either for yourself or for the person who has died, read on.

Earth or fire?

Burial and cremation are in many ways the opposite of each other, for all that the outcome of each is exactly the same. You have to face the facts of decomposition here, and it's not a pretty topic.

Cremation is rapid, fiery, hot, bright, dry, cheap and high-tech.

Burial is slow, earthy, cold, dark, soggy, expensive and low-tech.

Cremation is aggressive, brutal, unnatural. It trashes the body.

Burial is gentle, kind, natural. It respects the body.

Cremation is clean and odourless.

Burial is rotten and smelly.

You can pitch them against each other, but you'll never get a clear winner.

You can argue it any way you like. There's no resolving this with reason. It probably comes down to a gut feeling. Which sort of decomposition do you prefer?

It is interesting to note here that atheists, who take a materialistic view of the body and deny the existence of the spirit, will often express a strong preference for one or the other, even though, according to their belief system, it really couldn't matter less.

Which is cheaper?

Costs vary according to where you live, but cremation is almost always much less expensive than burial. Check out the prices in your local area. Type 'crematorium + your town' into your search engine.

Burial is more expensive in cities and cheaper in the country. Even then, the price is subsidized by profits made by the crematorium. The price can triple if the person who died was not a resident. The plot is yours for anything from 50 to 100 years. You don't buy it, you lease it.

8

Cremation

The popular way to go.

Reasons for.

Reasons against.

Everything you were afraid to ask.

Can you have an open-air cremation on a funeral pyre?

Cremation is the popular way to go. The figure in the UK stands at 70 per cent, the highest in Europe. Historically, cremation fell out of favour when Europe went Christian because religious leaders reckoned it would be impossible for ashes to be reconstituted as a human body on the day of resurrection. It came back into favour when graveyards started filling up and stinking. Church leaders had second thoughts. Cremation now saves around 200 acres a year.

For

It's cheaper than burial, the body doesn't take up space in a cemetery and you get to keep the ashes and do what you like with them.

Against

Nasty emissions from crematoria chimneys include CO^2, cancer-causing dioxins and mercury from vaporized amalgam fillings in teeth. Mercury is especially hazardous. It pollutes earth, air and water, notably the North Sea, where it is ingested by fish which are eaten by humans. Mercury damages the brain, the central nervous system and fertility. EU regulations are being introduced to halve emissions by 2012, adding around £100 to the cost of every cremation. Why not remove fillings before cremation? It's a notion many consider macabre. If only they knew how innocuously it compares with embalming and post-mortems.

The amount of energy required to cremate a body is equivalent to around a month's domestic energy consumption for a single person.

Ashes, also called cremated remains, are of little environmental value. They contain phosphorus, calcium and other nutrients that plants like. When scattered on, for example, Scottish mountainsides, they upset the ecology; when scattered on football pitches they upset the fans.

Is it really true that . . .

Even shrewd, sceptical, educated people easily believe that, behind the scenes in a crematorium, bodies are pulled out of coffins, coffins are taken away in the back of a van to be re-used, many bodies are cremated together, all packed in and folded like foetuses, and the ashes you get back are all mixed up. What really goes on?

What really goes on

Here is a typical, everyday, behind-the-scenes occurrence at a crematorium.

In the crematorium chapel, the service has just ended. 'Time to Say Goodbye' is still playing as the last of the mourners leave. There is tension in the air because the service has finished four minutes late and the mourners for the next service are building up outside. An attendant is hurriedly tidying hymn books and collecting up discarded service sheets. The curtain around the coffin draws back. The undertaker's men remove flowers from the coffin and take them out to the flower court where they can be admired. The undertaker in charge of the next funeral looks in, glances at his watch and shakes his head impatiently.

All this hurrying and scurrying in support of a process which sends people off into a place where time doesn't exist.

At a burial, you get to see the coffin reach its final destination at the bottom of a sur-prisingly deep hole. Not at a crematorium. When the curtains close, the coffin does not enter a fiery furnace. It doesn't go anywhere until you've gone.

There is a striking contrast between the décor of a crematorium chapel and the area behind the scenes, which has an industrial feel to it. Here, the technician opens a hatch and pulls the coffin, with just a single red rose on top, onto a steel trolley. Here the coffin stays and waits its turn.

When there is a free cremator, the technician checks her paperwork with the coffin plate, wheels the coffin to the cremator and opens its steel door. There's only room in there for one coffin. The firebricks glow red, but there are no flames. In goes the coffin. So great is the heat that flames flutter from the coffin. She shuts the door and the temperature rises to 850–1,000°C. This is a computer-controlled process. A name card records who is being cremated. At this crematorium the technician likes to preserve the privacy of the person being cremated, so she turns the card around so that no stranger can see who's in there.

It takes around 75 minutes to cremate a body and its coffin, which is reduced to a little ash and a few bone fragments. The technician carefully rakes them into a collecting tray and puts them aside to cool. Next, she runs a magnet over them to collect any metal fragments. If there were an artificial joint or plate, she'd pick it out and put it in a tin with others awaiting burial or recycling. Finally, she pours the cooled ash and fragments into a cremulator, a machine in which ball bearings rotate and grind the bone fragments to the consistency of grit. Grey-white grit, ready for collection. Most people reduce to between five and eight pounds of ash and are suitable for scattering almost anywhere or preserving in almost any form.

All cremations have to take place within 72 hours of the funeral. Most are done within a few hours.

The ashes you get are definitely the right ashes, no doubt about it. Find out what you can do with them in Chapter 42.

Burning zeal

Cremation as we know it is only just over a hundred years old. Its pioneers in the Cremation Society had to overcome all sorts of prejudice, most of it religious, some of it legal. Just when matters appeared to be at a stalemate, a most unlikely trailblazer appeared. Step forward Dr Price.

William Price first attracted attention as a schoolboy by reading poetry as he walked through the countryside naked. After qualifying as a doctor he became involved in revolutionary politics. He was a druid, given to wearing a red waistcoat, green trousers and a fox pelt on his head.

In 1883, when he was 80, he took as his lover a woman 60 years younger. With her he had a son whom he named Jesus Christ. Jesus died when he was five months old. In accordance with ancient druidical practice, Dr Price proceeded to burn his body. A horrified crowd gathered and snatched the body from the flames. Price was prosecuted. He was acquitted, and the judgement delivered that cremation is legal so long as no nuisance is caused to others.

By winning this landmark ruling, Dr Price secured the legal breakthrough the Cremation Society had been looking for. The first crematorium was built at Woking, and the first person to be cremated there was the pioneering Mrs Pickersgill.

Not a bad achievement for a doctor who refused to treat patients who smoked.

Everything you were afraid to ask

What clothing is allowed on the body?

Most crematoria say yes to ordinary clothes but no shoes. Clothing should be combustible but not highly volatile – so waders are out. Some crematoria are tightening up and insisting on organic clothing only.

What happens to the coffin handles?

They are burned, too. They are plastic.

How does the body burn?

From the outside in. First to go is the coffin, last your lungs. Your body is 70 per cent water, so it burns as the heat drives off the moisture. The prettiest part is when your flesh has been consumed, leaving your skeleton briefly incandescing.

Who burns fastest?

Women burn faster than men. It's the subcutaneous fat that does it. Thin people tend to burn more slowly than plump people; big people take longer than little people. People who die of cancer are slow burners.

Are some people too fat to be cremated?

People are getting larger, and crematoria are having to instal wider cremators to fit them in. It may not be possible to cremate a very large person in your local area, in which case you'll have to travel to a crematorium which can fit them in.

Do they use the heat from the cremators to keep the building warm?

No, in most crematoria the heat goes up the chimney. It used to be reckoned inappropriate to recycle it, but the recyclers are winning the argument.

Is it true that, when a body is being burned, the heat causes it to suddenly sit up, bursting through the coffin lid?

A favourite cremation myth, this. No truth in it at all. But as the heat drives the moisture from your tendons, your body may writhe a bit in slow motion.

Do heart pacemakers really explode?

Yes, with considerable force. This is why they are always removed first.

Can you stand in the car park after the funeral and watch the smoke?

No. Smoke is removed from waste gases. All you see is the faintest haze.

Can you ask to see the coffin go into the cremator?

No problem. Hindus and Sikhs do this as a matter of course. Ring the crematorium in advance and they'll be only too happy. They will limit the numbers, though.

Are people who work in a crematorium a bit weird?

Not at all. They tend to be very conscientious, extremely helpful and quite a lot nicer than most people.

Can I see for myself what they do?

Yes. Go to deathonline.net/disposal/cremation/process.cfm (it's Australian but it could be British) or go to YouTube and type 'cremation' into the searchbox.

Hold your fire!

As determination to save the planet ebbs and flows in the realization that we will all have to consume less, the hunt is on for something less gas guzzling than cremation.

Presently, two alternatives are attracting attention.

Resomation is a water-based process which reduces a body to soft bone, easily crumbled. The body, in a steel basket encased in organic fabric, is immersed in an alkaline solution and heated to 170°C under pressure, which dissolves the soft tissue. Mercury is easily extracted at the end, as are any artificial joints, which are rendered good as new. There are no nasty emissions, but there's a lot of sterile liquid – it smells slightly of soap – to be got rid of. Think of it as the liquid equivalent of what goes up the crematorium chimney. The bone powder can be treated in the same way as cremated remains.

•   Find out more. Go to resomation.com.

Cryomation uses liquid nitrogen to freeze the body, which is then fragmented, freeze dried and rendered rapidly compostable in a shallow burial. It is the greenest process devised, both in terms of energy input and emissions. It will appeal especially to people who want their dead body to be as environmentally beneficial as possible.

•   Find out more. Go to cryomation.co.uk.

Funeral pyres and Viking funerals

A crematorium is a clinical place in which bodies are burned privately by gas jets. Maybe you'd like a more earthy, elemental and spectacular ceremony, one where your body is consumed by leaping flames atop a proper funeral pyre surrounded by family and friends. Is this lawful?

Yes, it is. In 2009 the Home Secretary, Jack Straw, with the cultural sensitivity for which he is famous, opposed an appeal in the High Court brought by a Hindu guru, Davender Kumai Ghai, that he be allowed to practise his religion freely and be burned on a pyre. Straw's grounds were that, as a country, we would be 'upset and offended' and 'find it abhorrent that human remains were being burned in this way'. He prevailed. But in 2010 the Appeal Court unexpectedly overthrew this judgement in favour of Mr Ghai and anyone else who wants to be cremated on a pyre.

Just three problems. You have to do it in a building of some sort. You've got to get that past the planners. And then the method of burning past the sniffy people at the Department for Environment, Food and Rural Affairs.

Open-air cremation appeals instinctively to many people. It has heritage appeal, too: our ancestors practised it at Stonehenge. Indeed, our word 'bonfire' derives from the Old English 'bane-fire' – literally, bone fire.

9

Burial

_____

Reasons for.

Reasons against.

Cemeteries.

Burial at sea.

Burial on private land.

For

Natural and gradual. You can pack the coffin with things the dead person will need in the afterlife, and carry on looking after them by visiting their grave and talking to them as you tend it.

Against

Burial uses land and, when you think how many graves in cemeteries are no longer tended by the occupants' families and friends, and haven't been for years, this is arguably a waste of badly managed space. The cost of maintenance is an everlasting burden. Strimmers prevent the development of natural habitats and decapitate frogs. The cost of maintaining cemeteries in perpetuity arguably makes sense only if you believe in a Day of Resurrection.

God's acre

Everyone has the right, regardless of religious affiliation, to be buried in their local Church of England parish churchyard. But don't get your hopes up: most are full.

A conventional cemetery

In many towns and cities, cemeteries are underfunded low-life habitats, haunts of alco-popped teenagers and substance abusers. Neglected, leaning headstones fall and injure people, reminding us of the harsh truth that in most cases just ten years pass before no one visits any more. In many other countries you rent your grave on a short lease. In Holland, for example, you lease a grave for up to 35 years, after which your family has an option to extend or the bones are dug up and put in a communal grave.

Britons cling to the notion that it is their right to occupy a grave space until Doomsday, but it can't go on like this; the cemeteries will all be full in 30 years.

People talk of buying a grave, but you don't. You buy the exclusive right to burial in a particular plot, which you lease for anything between 50 and 100 years. In theory, that grave could be recycled after that period, but in practice our fearless legislators lack the courage to enable this to happen. The favoured method would be for any existing remains to be dug up, then reburied deeper, making room for a new burial on top, a practice called lift and deepen. It will have to happen.

In Greater London you can now be buried in a grave more than 75 years old if there is room on top of the existing tenant.

The deepest a grave can be safely dug is 12 feet (it depends on the soil and the water table), and it can accommodate up to three coffins, with a regulation six inches of soil between each coffin and two feet six of earth on top.

A natural burial ground

Natural burial is described in Chapter 6.

Can you help dig the grave?

Gravedigging is skilled, hard work and potentially perilous, especially in sandy soils. The sides can cave in and bury you alive. Most graves are dug by mechanical diggers. But if you would like to help in any way you can in the digging of the grave, speak to the people in charge. You will be given only a small part at best, but that may be better than no part at all.

Burial at sea

The sea bed is a romantic final resting place for those who loved the briny when they were alive.

Like all the best romantic ideas, sea burial is fraught with complication and difficulties, not to mention expense. That's why only around twenty of them happen every year.

You can do it only where there is no hazard to shipping, especially fishing vessels. These places are:

- The Needles, off the Isle of Wight.

- The waters south of Newhaven in Sussex.

- The waters off Tynemouth.

You need to obtain a licence from DEFRA or, if you are Welsh, from the National Assembly. It's free. It will tell you precisely what you have to do.

The body must be tagged in case it should accidentally be freed from the coffin and washed ashore. The coffin must be weighted and have many holes bored in it to let the water in.

If you are determined to pursue the notion:

* Read an account in the *Natural Death Handbook*.

* Go to mfa.gov.uk/environment/works/burial.

Burial in your own garden

It is a matter of fascination to many people to discover that they can bury someone in their own garden or land.

In a nutshell, the position is this:

* You don't need any official permission, but DEFRA will go after you if there is a chance that the body could contaminate water supplies.

* Accordingly, site the grave more than ten metres away from standing or running water, and 50 metres away from a well, borehole or spring.

* Watch out for underground pipes and cables.

* It doesn't matter how close the grave is to your neighbours, but they may not be overjoyed about it.

* Record the burial in your deeds (advisable).

* The value of your house could go down.

* If you sell up, you may not be able to visit the grave.

* The new owners may exhume the body.

If you want to carry your researches further, buy a copy of the *Natural Death Handbook*. The Natural Death Centre has been a pioneer in clarifying the law and establishing people's rights in this matter.

10

Decision time – burial or cremation?

Tick what you have chosen:

☐ Cremation.

☐ Burial in a cemetery.

☐ Burial in a natural burial ground.

☐ Burial in the garden.

☐ Burial on private land.

☐ Burial at sea.

11

What happens when we die?

What is death?
What happens next?
Yes, we start to decompose . . .

Death is both an event and a process. There comes an instant when a person stops breathing, and that is when we say they have died. You can record that instant precisely.

But before this instant the body will, unless death was instantaneous, have gone through a process of shutting down. After death, it goes on shutting down in the absence of oxygen to sustain it. The brain, for example, dies within seven minutes of the heart stopping, but skin goes on living for another 24 hours or so. Hair and nails go on growing, some people think. Actually, they don't. The skin recedes, giving that impression.

When someone dies, the process of decomposition begins at once. The body may look very still, but there is plenty going on inside.

Blood, no longer circulating, settles in the lowest parts of the body, causing blue blotches. Stiffening of the body – rigor mortis – begins within a few hours. It is caused by a build-up of lactate. It normally wears off after between 36 and 48 hours.

Microbes in the intestine which, in life, had been kept at bay by the immune system, start to spread throughout the body. At the same time, body tissue releases enzymes and other chemicals which start to break it down. In short, the body begins to digest itself from inside. Within hours brownish-red fluid from the stomach can start to trickle up through the nose and mouth. Around two days after death, gases can begin to build up in the stomach causing bloating. Skin may begin to turn blue or green. There may be a strong odour.

A variety of other factors influences the rate of decomposition. Big people normally decompose more rapidly than thin people. The presence in the body of certain sorts of medication, particularly drugs used to control the symptoms of cancer, can lead to a very rapid onset of decomposition.

There is no need to go into greater detail. The point is, a dead body is unstable, and the only way of delaying the process of decomposition is by either keeping it very cold or embalming.

You need to know this if you want the person who has died to be kept at home for any length of time.

You need to know this if you want to visit the person who has died at the undertaker's. Most bodies, if refrigerated, will remain presentable, but not always.

You need to know this if you want to play your part in looking after the body of the person who has died.

Why would you want to do that? Read on.

12

Caring for the body – why would you want to?

If you have cared for someone in life and as they lay dying, why would you want to stop when they are dead?

Do you want to complete the journey with them?

Caring for the body of the person who has died may be very distressing for you and do you more harm than good.

Or it may dispel some of the bleakness and fear that surround death and help you to come to terms with what has happened.

Why would you want to play a part in looking after the body of someone who has died?

Here's one way of looking at it.

The dying and the dead are attended to by many specialists. Medics superintend the expiration. Undertakers spirit away the corpse, secrete it somewhere, exhibit it (optional) in an alien and cheerless room at an administratively convenient time, then present it, boxed and borne by black-clad strangers, for a funeral handled by another specialist, a priest or a secular celebrant. The people who care *for* the dying and the dead are likely, all or most of them, to be well-meaning or self-important strangers. Those who care *about* the dying and the dead are powerless spectators.

The saying goodbye has become disconnected from the death. The living have been disconnected from their dying and their dead. That's why the reappearance of the body at the funeral many days after the death can be such shock.

But the life lived, the dying, the death, the time after the death, the funeral, the survivors' enduring commemoration of the life lived – all these are points on the same continuum. You can't make proper sense of them if you don't join them up.

If you have cared for someone in life, and as they lay dying, why would you want to stop when they are dead? Wouldn't you want to complete the journey with them? If you are reading this guide after someone has died, their body may already have been taken away by strangers to the hospital mortuary. How did you feel about that?

Consider these words of Thomas Lynch, a funeral director who is also a poet: 'Ours is a species which deals with death by dealing with our dead.'

Everyone has an instinctive horror of dead bodies, but this horror does not necessarily extend to the body of someone you love. A dead body is very different from a living body but, if you stay with it, it can also be very mysterious and beautiful. If you stay away from it, horror may start to creep up on you. Guilt may be a factor.

This is the case for self-empowerment and engagement; for reclaiming as much as you can from the specialists.

Having said which, caring for the body of someone who has died may be very distressing and do you more harm than good.

You must decide what is going to be best for you.

The case for playing your part

The extent to which you might want, or be able, to get involved in caring for the body of someone who has died will depend on how they died and how you have reacted to their death. It will also depend on how prepared you are. And that will depend on how much you've thought about it, and whether the two of you, you and your dead person, ever talked about it and planned for it.

It is a very big decision to make at a time of great grief.

If, say, someone has died suddenly in a car crash, you may understandably be overwhelmed by grief. This is quite different from the death of an old person, a parent, say, who has been fading over a period of time. For you, for family and for friends, as well as for that person, death may well have come as a merciful release at the end of a good life.

How involved you want to be in caring for them after death is a matter for you. Here is the case for a hands-on approach.

From now on, you are going to have to grow accustomed to living without this person. Getting involved in caring for their body will enable you to go on looking after them until there is no more looking after to be done. You may well find, if you do what you can, that this will be helpful in enabling you to accept what has happened, to come to terms with it, and to let the person go. Nothing can spare you from grief, but this may lessen it, dispel some of the bleakness and fear that surround death, and help you to make some sort of sense of what has happened. It may also help you to reconfigure your relationship with the person who has died – because relationships do not end at death.

Playing a part in caring for their body gives you something really important to do – more important than arranging catering and notifying the bank, for all that these things have to be done too. Above all, it puts you back in control.

It is no longer our custom to care for the bodies of our dead. It used to be perfectly normal and it remains perfectly normal in many other cultures. But it is observable that even in those communities which remember how things used to be done, there is no desire to return to the 'good old days'.

Read on to complete your understanding of what needs to be done. Then you will be able to decide how much you want to do.

13

Caring for the body – what needs to be done?

Where do undertakers keep their bodies?

What needs to be done?

You can do it all yourself.

Or job share with the undertaker at home.

Or job share with the undertaker at the funeral home.

Or do nothing.

The Natural Death Centre.

How you can care for the person who has died

Long ago, before there were undertakers, all but the very rich used to lay out their own dead and keep them at home until the day of the funeral. There was no alternative. The community used to gather round and help. The big difference between then and now is that in those days most funerals took place a few days after death. Nowadays, we normally have to wait for at least a week.

Looking after the body of someone who has died may be perfectly straightforward, but it may not be. It all depends how quickly the body deteriorates. The only specialized knowledge an undertaker has is how to look after dead bodies, and you would be brave to reject it.

The fact is that the body needs to be cared for. Here are your options:

- You can do everything yourself without the help of an undertaker.
- You can work in partnership with an undertaker.
- You can let the undertaker do everything.

Some funeral directors will not be happy about letting you help care for the body of the person who has died. They may regard it as an invasion of their professional domain. Others will enthusiastically say yes. In regions where there are large numbers of Muslims, funeral directors are used to this. Most Muslims wash and lay out the bodies of their dead.

Where do undertakers keep their bodies?

Whatever you decide, you will want to reassure yourself, if you engage an undertaker, that your dead person will be looked after as you wish.

Your undertaker will keep the body in their mortuary in a fridge or an air-conditioned room in which there may be other bodies. A mortuary has tiled walls and a clinical feel. It contains equipment for washing bodies and, perhaps, embalming them. There is a stainless-steel table on which bodies are prepared for their coffins.

Most undertakers keep their mortuaries spotless. Not all. Some have clean, agreeable front offices disguising a grubby muddle behind. They can easily get away with it because no one ever asks them if they can see where their dead person is going to be kept.

If you decide to use an undertaker, ask to have a look at their mortuary. The question may well cause astonishment but, of course, you have a perfect right. Arguably, you have a strong duty.

Your request may do more than just astound some undertakers. Chains of undertakers in large towns and cities operate satellite branches comprising an interview room and 'chapel of rest' but no mortuary. Bodies are not, as some clients fondly but ignorantly suppose, kept snug and safe somewhere behind the scenes. No, they are whisked off to a central mortuary, some miles away perhaps, where they join lots of other anonymous dead bodies. Such an undertaker cannot arrange for you to visit the person who has died at short notice. They have to arrange to have an overworked person bring the body out and then take it all the way back. Is this how you want the body of your loved one to be looked after?

What needs to be done?

In brief, looking after someone when they are dead involves:

- washing the body, laying it out and dressing it;
- keeping the body in conditions which will slow decomposition.

Washing and dressing a dead body takes at least two people. You can choose to do this at home or at a funeral home. It is easier than washing and dressing someone who is bedbound, but it is not for the squeamish. While you are doing it you must be prepared for some body fluids to be emitted. As you move the body during washing you will drive air from the lungs, and this may cause it to groan.

There are some things undertakers do which they think you are better off not knowing about. These are the technically difficult things like closing the mouth and shutting the eyes. Undertakers customarily do this in a way you might consider brutal and invasive. Dead people don't mind who does what to them, of course, but that's not the point. It's all about what you believe to be respectful and appropriate.

If you are not squeamish, read about what they do in Chapter 15 under the heading 'Setting the features'. If you don't think you want to know what they do, but you are against any invasive procedures, the jaw of your dead person can be supported and the eyes simply closed. You will need to talk this over with your funeral director and insist on gentle procedures only.

Here are four options for you to consider. Do not make any decisions yet.

Option one: bring the body home and do it all yourself

If you want to do everything yourself, keep the body at home and arrange a funeral you must:

1. be able to lay on transport capable of carrying a prone body;

2. get hold of a stretcher;

3. have the strength to lift a heavy weight;

4. have at least three other people to help you;

5. have the carpentry skills to make a coffin, or know someone who does. If you want to buy one, read Chapter 39;

6. be able to obtain plenty of ice, preferably dry ice and, if you can, a portable air conditioner, in order to keep the body cool;

7. have the skill and the courage to deal with the body if it gets leaky;

8. do all the paperwork to arrange for cremation or burial.

Some undertakers will be happy to work with you as a paid consultant and even lend you equipment.

Option two: job-share with the undertaker at home

You can lay out the person who has died at home with the undertaker's help. Keep the body there for a couple of days or for as long as you can. Then get the undertaker to take it away and keep it in his or her fridge until either the day before, or the day of the funeral itself.

Option three: job-share with the undertaker at the funeral home

Have the undertaker take away the body and keep it in his or her fridge. Go down to the funeral home and wash the body and put it in the coffin with the undertaker's expert help. You can take music with you, and candles, and family and friends.

If you like, ask the funeral director to bring the body home a day or two before the funeral.

Option four: do nothing

If you cannot face the task of washing and laying out the body of the person who has died, ask the undertaker to do it all for you. It is what undertakers are used to.

Embalming?

Whether you prefer option 2 or option 3, you may wish to have the body embalmed. This is not a job you can do yourself. You may or may not wish to witness it. Read all about embalming in Chapter 15 and decide for yourself. Warning: don't if you're squeamish.

The Natural Death Centre

The Natural Death Centre (NDC) is a charity which campaigns for change in social attitudes to death and dying.

The philosophy of the NDC grew out of that of the natural childbirth movement. The NDC believes that taking control and keeping interventions by strangers to a minimum improves the quality of dying for the dying person and its impact on his or her carers. In the matter of caring for the dead, it believes that taking control is therapeutic.

The NDC encourages and supports those who want to arrange environmentally friendly and inexpensive funerals, and it is behind the Association of Natural Burial Grounds – anbg.co.uk.

A hands-on approach to dealing with the dying and the dead strongly appeals to people of all sorts who know their own minds and like to do things their way.

The NDC publishes *The Natural Death Handbook*, which is full of practical advice and personal stories. It operates a telephone helpline and offers free advice on all aspects of death and funerals.

Contact the NDC: naturaldeath.org, phone: 0871 288 2098.

14

Caring for the body – doing it all yourself

Who would do it?

What do you need to know?

What could be difficult?

A home-based funeral is sometimes called a DIY funeral, a term many people find repellent. Let's call it a home funeral.

When someone dies, most public officials advise you on the assumption that you will want to use a funeral director. Some will express amazement that you want to do it all yourself, some may try to dissuade you, some will disapprove and some will try to stand in your way. If anyone tries to tell you it's against the law, put them right. You are the funeral director.

The more prepared you can be in advance, the better. To begin from a standing start will be really difficult.

Who would want to?

People who favour a home funeral tend to be the sort who plough their own furrow and may be regarded as non-conformists. They are resourceful. They are self-reliant. They are brave and probably stubborn. They are not squeamish. If you are, stop reading now.

If you feel strongly about letting strangers take your dead person away to do with them you know not what; if you feel strongly that it's your duty to care for them and spend time with them in death as in life; if you think you have the emotional and physical strength to enable you to do that, then you may well be prepared and equipped for the task.

It needs serious thought. Not only can it be difficult in itself, it may also be difficult to explain to friends and neighbours. It's an unconventional thing to do. Do you care?

What will your close family members and friends think? You will need their help. At least four of them, preferably six.

The Rule of Five

Before you can sensibly undertake any practical task in which you are unversed, you need five things.

1. An understanding of the difficulties.

2. An understanding of the worst that can go wrong.

3. The right equipment.

4. A workshop manual.

5. The phone number of an expert who can advise – or ride to your rescue in case of calamity.

Before we look at some of the difficulties, you may be sure that the paperwork involved is not one of them. It's a tedious doddle. Contact your local authority bereavement services officer. You will almost certainly find them both helpful and supportive.

Is no previous experience enough?

Looking after a dead body is a lot easier than looking after a bedridden adult or a helpless child. You can do it all from the workshop manual.

Undertakers don't do anything that you couldn't, in a way that a plumber, say, almost certainly can. The dead are wholly safe in the hands of amateurs so long as they (the amateurs) are up for it, for there's nothing you can do to a dead person in a well-intentioned way which that dead person will actually mind. Looking after our dead is not the exclusive preserve of a secular priesthood possessed of arcane knowledge.

Is it possible to keep a body at home for so long?

Perhaps nothing makes better sense of death than spending time with your dead person and becoming aware of one of death's great paradoxes: their present absence. One of the most therapeutic features of a home funeral is to observe the small changes that take place in the dead person over time. Nothing more effectively brings home the finality of death and reinforces the sense of the dead person's increasing physical distance from life. There will come a time when you know with serene certainty and acceptance that it's time for them to go.

You will start to feel this strongly after about three days, but it may not be possible to arrange a funeral that soon, definitely not a cremation, though your crematorium may be able to fit you in at short notice in their first slot of the day, a time unpopular with most people. The administrative process for burial is much faster.

In most cases, if you arrange to keep your dead person at home for no longer than a week, so long as you keep him or her cool all should be well. If it all goes wrong or gets too much you know what to do (see 5 below).

1. Some of the difficulties

If someone dies at home and there are no unexplained circumstances requiring a post mortem, a home funeral may be a relatively straightforward undertaking unless death happens shortly before Christmas, or when other public holidays may delay funeral arrangements.

Other difficulties may be:

1. Place of death.

2. Circumstances of death.

3. The condition of the body.

If there is a post mortem

If there has to be a post mortem (sometimes called an autopsy) you will not be able to have the body until it is released by the coroner. In routine cases that will be a few days, but it could be much longer.

When a post mortem is performed, the body is cut open so that organs can be examined. If the brain is examined, the top of the skull (from just above the ears) is removed. When the examination is over, the body is stitched up and the top of the skull stitched back on. This is often done without much care because funeral directors can disguise it. If you tell the coroner's office that you will be caring for the body yourself, the pathologist's assistants will almost certainly stitch far more thoughtfully.

Could you handle this?

Find out more by Googling 'post mortem procedure' or go to:

*   yourrights.org.uk. Type 'post mortem' into the searchbox. Excellent resource from human rights watchdog Liberty.

*   For a cartoon-illustrated description of a post mortem by a pathologist, go to pathguy.com/autopsy.

If the person has been in an accident

If the person has been in an accident, you may want to consider hiring a funeral director to help wash and dress the body, or even to handle all of that.

If the person dies away from home

If the person dies in a hospital, hospice or nursing home you will need to be able to bring the body home. To do this you will need a stretcher (unless the body is light enough, or that of a child), a helper and a vehicle big enough to carry the body. You will almost certainly encounter amazement if not opposition from officials.

You may find it easier to hire a funeral director to help you.

Is a dead body infectious?

If the person has died of a disease which would put you at risk, your doctor will tell you.

If the person has died of a notifiable disease, the Public Health (Control of Disease) Act empowers a doctor to prohibit the release of the body from a hospital, to forbid anyone from holding a wake over the body and to direct that the body be taken either to a mortuary or to be buried or cremated immediately. Notifiable diseases are listed on the Health Protection Agency website: hpa.org.uk.

Most viruses and diseases can survive no longer than a few hours in a dead body.

The micro-organisms associated with decomposition are not the kind that cause disease. Smells don't kill.

Almost all dead bodies are not dangerous. Gloves and simple protective clothing are all you need – and a mask, if you like.

2. The very worst that can happen

According to Erika Nelson, a funeral director, quoted in the *Crossings Manual for Home Funeral Care* (see below) the following conditions make a body especially difficult to care for:

- Bed sores – open wounds which leak fluid.
- Oedema – fluid-filled blisters.
- Obesity.
- Certain infections.
- Septicaemia.
- Rapid decomposition.

A number of factors govern the rate of decomposition even when the body is kept cool. Those which may hasten it include: the duration of the dying process; cause of death; the size of the body; the contents of the stomach; and the presence of medication (especially cancer drugs). A nurse may be able to offer an opinion. Sometimes, decomposition can progress very fast (see 5 below).

3. The right equipment

Chances are that you have almost all the equipment you need in the house already – towels, sheets, etc. What you're doing, remember, is as old as time itself.

You'll need to keep the body cool and you do that with ice packs – the sort you use for picnics. It will take 48 hours the first time you do it, so get them in as early as you can. Dry ice is an expensive alternative fraught with handling difficulties.

You'll need to keep the room cool, so a portable air-conditioning unit is a desirable extra.

You'll need a coffin, which you can either make yourself or buy. See Chapter 39.

You will need strong and willing hands to help you.

4. A workshop manual

There is presently no home funeral care manual dedicated to people in the UK. The only resource published here is the *Natural Death Handbook* which, though helpful, is not comprehensive.

From the USA, where the home funeral movement is thriving, you can obtain two excellent resources, both of which have informed this chapter. Both are detailed and both are downloadable from the internet. Both contain accounts of home funerals which will also be informative and, perhaps, also inspiring. If what you have read so far has not deterred you, go to:

•   Crossings.net.

•   Homefuneralmanual.org.

If you'd like to see what a home funeral looks like, go to:

•   flickr.com/photos/homefunerals.

5. Phone a friend

Many funeral directors will be happy to stand by and help you out if it all gets too much – for a fee, of course. Most won't feel professionally miffed, though they'll be aware of lost revenue, of course. But many will actually approve and be enthusiastically supportive.

Many funeral directors will be happy to act as consultants throughout the process, and drop in whenever you want to check that all is well.

15

Embalming

WARNING: not for the squeamish!

A brief history of embalming.

Embalming today.

Is embalming really necessary?

What do the embalmers say?

The value of embalming.

Green issues.

What exactly do embalmers do?

Setting the features.

Embalming is a subject which arouses strong feelings. Some people consider it horrible and unnecessary. Others, especially if they want to spend a lot of time with their dead person, are very grateful for it.

Undertakers are reluctant to go into detail about what is involved. Sometimes they don't call it embalming at all. They call it 'hygienic' or 'sanitary' treatment instead. These are misleading terms. You probably think this has got something to do with washing the body. Of course you do not want your dead person's body to be un-hygienic, so, when it's offered, you say yes, please do it.

You have effectively been lied to.

The reason why undertakers do not go into detail about embalming is because it is eyebrow-raisingly invasive. The end of this chapter will tell you precisely what happens, but you will be warned when you get there. You will need a strong stomach.

First, a bit of background.

A brief history of embalming

Think Pharaoh. Think again. Present-day embalming isn't a bit like that.

Ancient Egyptians embalmed bodies because their religion told them to. The bodies of the nobility were, first, eviscerated, then dried, softened with sweet-smelling ointments – the balms which give us the word – stuffed and bandaged. Mummified.

Achieving an illusion of aliveness was never the point. The point of preservation was to render a body forever recognizable to its departed soul because, one day, that soul would return, wishing to resume occupancy.

In Christian Europe religious teaching forbade embalming. Resurrection was guaranteed to all who had lived virtuous lives, not just those who could produce a halfway recognizable corpse as their ticket of admission on the Day of Judgement.

Kings and queens were sometimes embalmed because it took so long to get around to burying them – all that lying in state. Some Crusaders who wanted to be buried at home were embalmed. Horatio Nelson's body was pickled in a keg of brandy.

Down the centuries various eccentrics dabbled in keeping bodies alive-looking with variably durable results. The best results were achieved entirely accidentally – the Bog People of northern Europe, for example, discovered tanned but amazingly lifelike in peat bogs 2,000 years after their death. They dug one up in Cheshire in 1984 and dubbed him Pete Marsh. They dug up a woman's head, jolting a local man to come clean about murdering his wife. When he heard, he thought it must be hers.

The breakthrough in the modern age happened in the USA at the time of the American Civil War with the invention of arterial embalming – draining the blood from the body and, using the arterial system, replacing it with chemicals. This made it possible for the bodies of those killed in battle to travel home for burial.

Embalming today

Because embalming delays decomposition and renders a dead body especially presentable it has become the custom in the USA to display the newly dead in funeral homes at a social event called a visitation. Not only is the body embalmed, it is also 'cosmetized' in order to leave those who see it with a pleasing 'memory picture'. This is a practice reckoned sentimental, icky or worse in most of the rest of the world, and it is banned by some religions and cultures, notably Jews and Muslims.

In the UK many funeral directors like to embalm because it enables them to display the person who has died to their family looking much more serene and peaceful than they did just after death. This, funeral directors reckon, reflects well on their duty of care and earns them gratitude. When it comes their own turn to die, interestingly, many of them ask for it not to be done.

Not all people are pleased with the effects of embalming. Sometimes the embalming is not well done and the face of the person who has died is too plumped up. Sometimes it is a weird shock to see the person who has died looking so much better, younger even, than they did just before they died.

As far as the undertaker is concerned, an embalmed body is much easier to look after, so there's a big convenience factor, too.

The effects of embalming typically last only a few days, though it is possible to achieve a longer-lasting result with bodies donated to medical science.

We all rot in the end. Even the expertly embalmed Lenin, these days, has to be held together by a wetsuit.

One thing present-day embalming has in common with the practices of ancient Egypt: it is invasive.

And it takes great skill.

Is embalming really necessary?

If you want to send someone's body abroad or bring someone's body back to this country, you must have it embalmed. That's the law.

For all other purposes embalming is, arguably, completely unnecessary.

You might consider it if any of the four following circumstances apply to you.

1. The body is going to spend long spells out of refrigeration.

    *   Your child or your lover has died and you want to spend as much time as you can with them.

    *   You want to have the body at home.

2. The person died in an accident.

    *   Your son has died in a motorcycle crash and was badly injured. The embalmer will be able to cover up some of the injuries (probably with wax) and restore the features.

3. The person who has died has begun to show signs of decomposition, especially discolouration, and you wish to spend time with them.

4. There is going to be a long time until the funeral.

    *   You have booked and paid for a holiday. You want to postpone the funeral until you get back in a fortnight's time. Embalming may be the only way of arresting decay, though some funeral directors would dispute this. Freezing would do the trick, but most undertakers' fridges do not have a freezer compartment.

If you simply want to go to the undertaker's to spend spells of an hour or two with the person who has died, embalming is unnecessary unless you favour the improved appearance that embalming can achieve.

If you do not wish to visit the body, embalming is entirely unnecessary.

Some funeral directors strongly dislike it; they do it only when they have to. Some love it and embalm every body they can.

What do the embalmers say?

Embalmers, of course, hotly dispute any assertion that their work is a waste of time and formaldehyde (the principal chemical used).

Trained embalmers in Britain are members of the British Institute of Embalmers (BIE). The BIE would have us believe that there are three reasons for embalming:

1. To prevent any danger to public health

There is a danger to public health when someone dies of a notifiable disease. But embalmers are not allowed anywhere near any body who has died of a notifiable disease, so embalming does not, therefore, prevent danger to public health.

2. To retard the process of decay

The BIE is right about this – embalming does retard decay by killing or halting micro-organisms – but a fridge usually does the job just as well in the short to medium term.

3. To restore a more lifelike appearance

The big reason for embalming is to make a dead person look, if not more lifelike, then less dead. There is never any mistaking that someone is dead; there's a motion-lessness about them and an absence of self which is nothing like sleep.

An embalmer can take a body which looks hollow and sunken and discoloured – hardly recognizable, perhaps – and in anything from an hour and a half to five hours make it look serene and peaceful and as you remember.

All undertakers strive to achieve this effect, not just embalmers. It is a cosmetic effect. The principal skill lies in what they call 'setting the features', arranging the face so that it looks reposeful. The features of a dead person are quite malleable whether embalmed or not.

Embalming, done well, will almost always produce a better appearance because it plumps up sunken, hollow features. What's more, it puts colour back into the skin.

Anyone who has died of disease or long illness or a traumatic event will usually look decidedly the worse for it. A heart attack, for example, will cause purple discoloration of the face; jaundice will leave a person yellow. Embalming them will restore lifelike skin colour because the chemicals are dyed. Some acute discolouration will fade naturally from the face as the blood sinks under the influence of gravity, but embalming will always counteract paleness.

Convenience embalming

In addition to these three reasons for embalming, the BIE might have added a fourth. Convenience.

Those undertakers who only use refrigeration must look after their bodies carefully. A quickie embalming renders a body much more stable. You can leave it out of the fridge for longer. The industry terms for a quickie embalming are 'hygienic treatment' and 'sanitary treatment'.

In something like half an hour an embalmer will be able to get a fair amount of chemical into the system, especially the face. A quick slosh around with the trocar and all's done: the body will remain conveniently decay-resistant and well behaved until the day of the funeral.

What's a trocar? Read: 'What exactly do embalmers do?' (see below) – but, be warned: only if you've got the stomach for it.

The value of embalming

Most embalmers are passionate about the value of what they do.

It takes from one-and-a-half to five hours to embalm a body properly, sometimes longer. A body which has had a post mortem may be especially difficult because there will be a lack of joined-up arteries. Good embalmers take immense pride in their work, painstakingly massaging fluid into the remotest parts, down to the fingertips. They are true craftspeople.

The best will skilfully reconstruct someone whose body has been badly injured in, say, a car crash. Using wax, they will cover wounds and 'mend' a skull.

They are skilled hairdressers and most are adept in the use of cosmetics.

Look at it this way. Your last memory of the person who died was when death happened. Maybe that's an unhappy, even horrific, memory. Every time you shut your eyes, that's what you see.

An expertly embalmed body will overlay that memory with one which is reassuring and comforting.

That effect combined with your gratitude is the embalmer's reward.

Here's another way of looking at it. Embalming is highly intrusive. Is that last, comforting picture really worth the price?

Decide for yourself.

Green issues

Most natural burial grounds say no to embalmed bodies, as you might expect. They don't like the chemicals.

However, there is no indisputable evidence that embalming fluid does the environment any lasting harm. Formaldehyde, the principal ingredient, evaporates, leaving no trace behind. There is growing evidence, though, that it is very bad for embalmers, who often have to work in unventilated rooms. The fumes sear the noses of some and cause dizziness. They may be carcinogenic.

The green way to embalm is with Aardbalm, a non-toxic alternative to formaldehyde-based products. It's not popular, though, with most embalmers.

Why would anyone become an embalmer?

Why would anyone become an embalmer, you wonder. A great many undertakers wonder this, too, as a matter of fact.

Of course, the trade attracts the odd weirdo but most embalmers are perfectly ordinary and nice. They do what they do because, as we've seen, it makes people happy. It's the service element that really turns them on, together with immense pride in their handiwork, for it is very skilled work indeed. It is also surprisingly badly paid.

It's an unregulated trade, of course. Anyone can set themselves up as embalmer. To ensure best service, insist that your undertaker uses a trained BIE member. Look out for the initials MBIE. The membership certificate for this Cinderella service is the most impressive of them all. The BIE website is a useful source of information:

* bioe.co.uk.

What exactly do embalmers do?

WARNING! What follows is a blow-by-blow account of an embalming. Read on only if you think you'll be able to stomach it.

Embalmers like to get their hands on a body as soon as possible. If it's still warm, so much the better because the blood will not have begun to coagulate. Embalmers hate clots.

Having washed the body with antiseptic soap, the embalmer makes an incision into an artery. Each has their favourite, perhaps the carotid artery (at the junction of neck and shoulder) or the femoral artery (in the groin). Next, the embalmer inserts a tube connected to a pump connected to a reservoir full of embalming fluid. Then the embalmer cuts into another artery close to the heart, the jugular, perhaps, and inserts a tube through which blood can drain.

Embalming fluid is pumped in, a mixture of formaldehyde, borax, glycerin, phenol, potassium nitrate, acetate dye and water. As the pump pushes fluid into the body, so it pushes blood out through the drain vein, thick and dark at first, then thinner as it dilutes.

As the embalming fluid irrigates an arm, the vessels stand out. As it flows around the face, the features become fuller and harder. The knack is to mix the chemicals so that the features do not become too hard and bloated. Those areas which have not received their full share of fluid can be treated with shots from a hypodermic syringe.

Getting the blood out is seldom that easy. In most bodies, by the time the embalmer gets them, the blood will have started to coagulate. It needs to be coaxed. Massaged. The body must be shaken and rocked. A good way to shift it is to bring down a clenched fist heavily on the breastbone. If all else fails, the embalmer pushes a trocar into the heart and drains direct from there.

A trocar is a long metal pipe attached to a tube attached to a machine that sucks.

It's not over. Stomach contents decompose, causing a build-up of repugnant gases and what undertakers call purge: browny-red liquid which oozes through the mouth and nose. The embalmer pushes a trocar into the belly, just above the navel, sloshes about and sucks out as much as can be reached. All the organs are pierced. What emerges? Blood, food, faeces, urine and bits of tissue. The chest cavity may be treated to some of the same treatment. When all's done, the trocar is connected to a bottle of embalming fluid and the stomach and chest cavities gravity-filled.

Job almost done. The embalmer now disposes of everything sucked out. Some will have to use the toilet. It all goes into the mains drainage. No danger to public health, then.

Last comes the fun bit: washing the hair, applying cosmetics and making the corpse look nice and well-dressed.

The handiwork will, with luck, last until the day of the funeral. When the body is buried, it will soon begin to decompose.

Setting the features

Even undertakers who disapprove of embalming will routinely do things to a body which may leave you aghast. They will not ask your permission, so you must get your decision in first. These things involve closing the eyes and the mouth.

On TV shows and in movies you are accustomed to seeing horrifically mutilated corpses, but the directors seem to think that you will not be able to bear to see their mouths gaping. In real life it is very difficult to keep the mouth of a dead person shut. They're always shut in *Silent Witness*. That's how you know they're not dead.

What's more, most people's eyes stay open in death.

How do you close them?

Most undertakers shut the eyes by using eye caps. An eye cap is a plastic hemisphere dimpled on the outside. The eyelid is pulled up, the eye dried, the cap put on top of the eyeball and the eyelid pulled over it. This has the virtue also of plumping up the eyeballs, which sink in death.

Undertakers close the mouth by means of what they call a jaw suture: a long stitch made inside the mouth with a curved, threaded needle through the bottom lip beneath the teeth, up under the top lip, through the septum and back down into the mouth. A simple knot then pulls the jaw shut, the trick being not to tie it too tight – it creates a parrot expression. Lips ever so slightly parted is reckoned the best look.

If you find either of these procedures objectionable it is possible to keep eyes closed by either pulling the top lid over the lashes of the lower lid, or coating the edges with Vaseline. It is possible to keep the jaw shut by supporting it underneath the chin or by tying it shut with a bandage knotted over the top of the head.

Alternatively, you can simply leave the jaw open.

Be sure to tell your undertaker what he or she may or must not do.

Looking like death

Most people don't reckon to look their best when they're dead, but this was not how the status-conscious citizens of Palermo in Italy saw it.

Starting in 1599 the Capuchin friars were mummified or embalmed, then displayed, standing, in the catacombs beneath their friary. The idea appealed to the wealthy citizens of Palermo, who clamoured to join them. Permission was granted and, over the centuries, their numbers grew and grew. The custom was only discontinued in the 1920s.

There to this day they stand or sit or lie, gathered according to profession, wearing the clothes they wore in life. They now constitute a fascinating record of social history – and an object of macabre fascination to goggling tourists.

Around 8,000 desiccated corpses gregariously survive in varying states of repair, their expressions altered over time, many of them now seeming silently to be singing in chorus, nattering, making merry or expostulating. One of the last to be entombed was a child, Rosalia Lombardo, who remains to this day touchingly well preserved.

See them at: members.tripod.com/~Motomom/index-3.html.

16

Going to see someone who has died

Why would you want to do it?

Why would you not want to?

Arranging your visit.

If you choose to have the person who has died looked after at the undertaker's, you may well want to visit them.

Spending time with a person who has died is something some people want to do and others don't. There's no right or wrong about this. Sometimes, when a person dies suddenly, you will hear their family say, 'I can't believe she's gone. I keep expecting her to walk in through the door.' They wouldn't say this if they went and spent some time with the body.

Until undertakers professionalized the care of the dead, it was the custom to hold a vigil or wake over the dead, often round the clock.

Why would you want to do it?

Visiting someone who has died gives you:

- time to accept what has happened;
- time to let go;
- time to take in the fact that your world has changed;
- time to say what you have to say;
- time to see that person looking peaceful, not as they were when they had just died.

If you think it's a difficult thing to do, consider this: people who do it are often the better for it.

Why would you not want to do it?

- Because you don't want to see the person dead.

- Because you don't need to.

- Because the body was too badly injured.

If the body has been badly injured

If the body has been badly injured, you can still go and visit. Your funeral director may be able to make the body presentable. If not, you can arrange for the body to be covered except for, say, a hand. Or you can arrange to have the coffin covered, and simply sit beside it.

Arranging your visit

This is what happens. The undertaker puts the coffined body in what he or she calls a chapel of rest or a viewing room – a small, dimly lit room decorated often in questionable if not revolting taste in which there may be religious symbols or paintings. Some undertakers will put the body on a bed if you wish. If you want religious images removed, say so before you go.

Undertakers call this 'viewing', a peculiar and inappropriate word. When in your life did you ever go and view anybody? Tell the undertaker you want to visit. Or come and see.

In the UK, visiting the dead is a private matter. The undertaker will only allow visitors approved by the person arranging the funeral.

After you have gone, the undertaker will put the body back in the fridge.

If you want to spend a long time with the person who has died, you must make this clear when you first contact the undertaker. Some undertakers will not be able to give you as much time as you need. If the body is going to have to spend a lot of time out of the fridge, the undertaker may suggest embalming. Some undertakers will strongly suggest embalming even if you only want to visit once. This is something other undertakers would disagree with. To respond to this you must sort out your views on embalming. See Chapter 15.

Coming home

If you want to spend time with the body at home, the day before the funeral is probably the best.

17

Decision time – caring for the body

Tick what you have decided to do:

- ☐ Option one: bring the body home and do it all ourselves.
- ☐ Option two: job share with the undertaker at home.
- ☐ Option three: job share with the undertaker at the funeral home.
- ☐ Option four: sub-contract everything to an undertaker.
- ☐ Yes to embalming.
- ☐ No to embalming.
- ☐ Yes to mouth suture and eye caps.
- ☐ No to mouth suture and eye caps.
- ☐ I do not want to visit.
- ☐ I want to visit once.
- ☐ I want to visit for long periods.
- ☐ I want to visit every day.
- ☐ I want to visit once, on the day before the funeral.
- ☐ I want all religious imagery to be taken out of the chapel of rest.

18

Style your funeral

What sort of a ceremony do you want?

Religious, semi-religious or non-religious?

A celebration of life?

What will people think?

We don't believe in God. What are our options?

We don't go to church. Can we have a hymn and some prayers?

How do I find a celebrant?

Does it have to be at the crematorium?

Dad didn't want a funeral. Do we have to abide by his wishes?

Should children come to the funeral?

Religious, semi-religious or non-religious?

Before you begin to start looking for a funeral director, it is a good idea to decide what sort of a funeral ceremony you want to have.

If you have already decided that you want a full religious funeral, you know exactly what to expect. Skip this chapter.

For everyone else, here's a remarkable statistic. Around 90 per cent of people do not go to a place of worship regularly, yet most of them choose to have a religious funeral. The Church of England performs four times as many funerals as weddings. Why?

Because arranging a funeral is something most people only have to do once or twice in their lifetime. When you are not skilled and experienced at doing something, you understandably lack the confidence to strike out on your own. The most important thing, you feel, is to do the right thing: what's expected. So you ask yourself, 'What does everyone else do?'

And the answer is that almost everyone opts for a full religious funeral. It's still the done thing, the default option. You can see why. Most people do not reject religion outright – the number of full-blown atheists is very small. Many people find great comfort in the rituals, music and language of a religious ceremony, in which there is likely to be more beauty, poetry and audience participation than you will find in any non-religious ceremony. All religions have long experience of putting on a really good show, many of them in a stunning architectural setting.

What's more, people feel they must have a proper, official person to conduct a funeral and make it valid: a priest.

When it comes to religion, most people are don't-knows. Or their faith is hazy. They lead decent lives on the whole, go to a place of worship occasionally, perhaps, and are happy to take a chance on what happens when they die. If there is a hereafter, great; if there isn't, oh well. A religious service can seem like a good insurance policy just in case there is.

For people like this a religious funeral may, though, miss the point. It can alienate those who come to the funeral to have to listen to a lot of dogma they haven't signed up to. The Church of England, in particular, comes in for a lot of deserved criticism for the way some of its priests conduct funerals, but you've got to look at things from their point of view, too: it is hard for a priest to engage with an audience which glares back with empty or hostile eyes. It is difficult to imagine the deity being all that impressed, either.

Your funeral doesn't have to be like this. There is a better way. Priests are not the only proper people to conduct funerals.

Let's start thinking about what's going to be right for you.

A celebration of life

Non-religious and semi-religious funerals are growing in popularity because they do what people want: they focus on the life of the person who has died and give thanks for that life. They are tailor-made to accord with that person's beliefs and those of their family, so they are much more individual than a religious ceremony, which puts God first and has a fixed format to which you can contribute very little.

Better still, you, the organizer, have complete control over what happens. If you want the funeral to be a celebration of life, that's what you can have – exactly as you want it.

You can create the funeral from scratch or you can engage an expert, a secular *celebrant*, to work with you and advise.

The best and the worst

First, think of any funerals you have been to.

What was good about the best?

What was bad about the worst?

Jot them down.

Now read on and consider alternatives to the 'traditional' religious funeral.

What's your style?

A funeral can be as elaborate or as simple as you want. The style of funeral you favour will be determined by the tastes and values of those organizing it and by the way people feel about the death. Take a pencil and tick what describes you.

Tradition

Would you describe yourself as:

☐ a traditionalist;

☐ someone who likes tradition with a modern twist;

☐ a modernist;

☐ an innovator;

☐ a mould-breaker – a bit of an anarchist.

Formality

Thinking of the sense of occasion you want to create, do you want the funeral to be:

☐ formal;

☐ smart;

☐ informal, spontaneous?

Ceremonial

Do you like ceremonial? In a funeral this might include a horse-drawn hearse, a procession, a military salute, a particular and elaborate ritual.

☐ Lots.

☐ Some.

☐ None?

Mood

The mood of the funeral will mostly be determined by how people feel towards the person who has died. Do you expect the mood to be:

☐ angry;

☐ guilty;

☐ shocked;

☐ sombre and regretful;

☐ one of acceptance;

☐ grateful, happy and celebratory?

Participation

What part would you like those who come to the funeral to play? In evaluating this, ask yourself what part you think they'd like to play.

☐ Anyone who wants should be able to say or do what they want, and we will make time for this.

☐ We want only invited people to take part.

☐ The ceremony will be led by just one person.

Poetic or plain?

You may want the funeral to appeal to the *minds* of those who come, or you may want it to appeal to their *senses*, or you may want it to do *both*. Which?

☐ Rational. Prosaic. Logical. Plain words, plain speaking, down to earth, no nonsense.

☐ Sensuous. Spiritual. Evoking a sense of mystery and wonder through poetic writings, images, music and ritual.

☐ A bit of both.

Structure

Do you think the funeral ceremony ought to be:

☐ firmly structured, with no deviation from that structure;

☐ structured, but with some scope for spontaneity;

☐ unstructured and wholly spontaneous?

Cost

Do you want the funeral to be

☐ costly;

☐ mid-range;

☐ as inexpensive as possible?

Environmental

Do you want the funeral to:

☐ make the smallest possible impact on the environment;

☐ keep its environmental impact to an acceptable minimum;

☐ go ahead without any consideration at all for its environmental impact?

What will people think if we have a non-religious funeral?

If a non-religious or semi-religious funeral seems to you to be an unconventional and therefore a risky option which people coming to the funeral may be unhappy about, don't worry. Most people vastly prefer them.

Won't a funeral without a priest lack dignity?

You know that the people who are coming to the funeral will expect it to be dignified. What makes for dignity?

A dignified funeral can range in style from a highly structured royal funeral full of pomp and pageantry to an unstructured Quaker funeral. A dignified funeral can be highly formal or stripped-down simple.

Any ceremony, however formal or informal, is dignified so long as it is sincere and meaningful.

So: do what is right for you, for the person who has died, and for those close to him or her.

A good funeral is one where people say what they need to say, do what they need to do and spend all the time it takes to do that.

Tell me more about a Quaker funeral

Quakers are Christians, but you don't have to be religious to have a Quaker-style funeral.

Instead of interspersing periods of speech with intervals of silence, which is the normal way of funerals, Quakers do it the other way round. A Quaker funeral is unplanned, unstructured and very simple. Everyone sits in meditative silence, sometimes in a circle with just a candle in the middle. There are no readings and there is no eulogy. Instead, people talk about the person who has died spontaneously as the spirit moves them – and then the silence starts again. The end is determined by someone appointed beforehand who stands and shakes hands with a neighbour, whereupon everyone shakes hands – or holds hands. And then they leave.

We actively don't believe in God. What are our options?

Only one faith group does not sign up to an afterlife. Atheists believe there is no God (they can't prove it). An atheistic funeral is normally called a *humanist funeral*. It asserts the non-existence of God. You live, you die: that's it.

If the person who has died was a passionate atheist with a strong dislike of all organized religions, the funeral ceremony is an occasion when you may wish to proclaim that belief and deny the existence of an afterlife. The danger here is that you could make religious people feel excluded. But if you include in the funeral a period of silence where everyone can think about the person who has died, and religious people can offer up a silent prayer for them, you can bring them back in.

In this way, a humanist funeral can be inclusive in a way a religious funeral cannot.

A humanist funeral is very person-centred. It looks back over the life of the person who has died and celebrates it.

The British Humanist Association offers a network of trained and accredited celebrants nationwide to help you create the funeral ceremony and be MC on the day if you wish. They call them celebrants.

We don't go to church much. Can we still have a hymn and some prayers?

If you are not a regular worshipper you may feel it would be hypocritical or just uncomfortable to have a priest – a stranger in strange clothing – running the show.

And yet many people like to incorporate spiritual elements into their funeral ceremony, and for all sorts of reasons. Just because someone never goes to church does not mean that they have rejected all spiritual beliefs.

Will some religious people be coming to the funeral? Do you feel you ought to include some prayers for their benefit? Do you just happen to like the old hymns and reckon a funeral won't be a funeral without them?

You don't need a priest to lead a service which has a hymn and some prayers, and there is no part of a funeral ceremony which needs a priest to make it valid. You can do it all yourself or you can engage a celebrant to lead it for you.

How do I find a celebrant?

Find out more about celebrants in Chapter 20.

Does it have to happen at the crematorium?

All crematoria have a space where you can hold a funeral ceremony. The fee for this is bundled with the charge, whether you use it or not. You don't have to. You can arrange to hold a funeral at your home, in the pub, at the beach. Find out more in Chapter 19.

Our problem is, there was no love lost

Are you arranging a funeral for someone whom you and the rest of your family did not like much? Examples may include a physically abusive parent, a long-term alcoholic or someone who never much liked you.

Most people do not like to speak ill of the dead, but feel that to hold a funeral where the person who has died is talked about in glowing terms would be hypocritical.

If this is your position, that person has, inevitably, played a significant part in your life. You may think that, whatever your feelings, it is an important principle and duty to mark the passing of a human life.

If that is how you feel, you may wish to hold a funeral which does not talk much about the life of the person who has died. A religious funeral will do this. If you want a humanist or a semi-religious funeral, both of which are customarily centred on the life of the person who has died, you can create a shorter ceremony in which silent thought and reflection take the place of words.

You can, of course, create a ceremony in which you and others vent your anger and disappointment and describe how the behaviour of the person who has died affected you. This may be cathartic. On the other hand, you may, later, come to regret it.

Dad didn't want a funeral, but we want to have one for him. Do we have to abide by his wishes?

Many people do not want their family and friends to have to undergo the ordeal of a funeral because, understandably, they don't want their nearest and dearest getting upset on their account. Some say things like 'Just put me in a bin bag and dump me in a skip.'

Is that what they would have done to you?

If you know that the person who has died did not want a funeral, yet you want to have one for them, go ahead and have one. It won't do them any harm, and it'll do you a lot of good.

It's not the place of dead people to tell you how you should be feeling. Pay no attention. Give them the send-off you think they deserve.

We want to have a private, invitation-only, family funeral

If you want to have a funeral to which only selected people are invited, that's your right.

A private funeral will be a more intimate event. You won't be on public display. You can do what you want to do without having to accommodate the expectations of those you don't want to be there.

You will need to balance this against the consideration that in doing so you may be denying other people the opportunity to do what may be very important to them: to pay their respects and say goodbye. This could cause hurt and resentment.

You can follow a private funeral with a public memorial service in which everyone can participate. Again, you have to make a careful judgement: will this be adequate, or will it be too little, too late?

Should children come to the funeral?

Many people think it's wrong for children to be taken to a funeral. It's reckoned to be emotionally too gruelling for them and may leave them with horrible memories.

If you are a parent struggling with this problem, you know your child best.

If you think your child should not go, you need to have reasons. These reasons could include:

- Not wanting your child to have to confront death just yet.

- Not wanting your child to see adults, including yourself, upset.

- Not wanting your child to see a coffin.

In fact, children tend to be far more matter-of-fact and far less sentimental than adults and, being crammed with vitality, far less scared of death. They are arguably better prepared emotionally.

They are also curious creatures. To keep your child away from the funeral is to keep your child in ignorance. When a child is not given the facts, and not allowed to see, an overactive imagination can kick in and spawn a far more macabre and horrific parallel reality – a funeral full of ghosts and ghouls and God knows what.

To prepare your child for the funeral you will need to answer questions first, and you will need to supply answers appropriate to his or her age. These questions include:

- What happens when someone dies?

- What do dead people look like?

- Where do they go?

- What are they doing now?

- What will happen at the funeral?

- What happens when you're buried or cremated?

- How will other people behave at the funeral?

- How am I supposed to behave?

Only a parent can know whether or not their child should come to the funeral.

The solution to the dilemma 'Yes or no?' is yes. Always yes. If you come down firmly on the side of no, the answer is still yes.

Try to involve your child or children in the funeral ceremony. Get them to write a letter to the person who has died and have it put in the coffin. Involve them in a candle-lighting ceremony at the funeral. Write down their memories of the person who has died and incorporate what they say in the tribute.

Life is a succession of beginnings and endings. Nothing reinforces this sense of renewal better than the presence of those beginning their lives at a ceremony to celebrate someone whose life has ended. It is the most natural thing in the world.

Read on

Now that you have read this section, you are probably closer to knowing what sort of shape you would like the funeral to have. Don't make final decisions just yet. Read on.

19

The crematorium and other funeral venues

What are crematoria like?

Why do you get so little time?

Where else can we have the funeral?

Most people who do not want a church funeral favour the crematorium as their funeral venue. A crematorium is a building which offers two facilities: a ceremonial space for holding funerals – a chapel, if you like – and an incinerator for burning bodies. One fee covers both.

The crematorium is not just for people who opt for cremation. You can hold a ceremony here prior to a burial. You pay the same.

People favour the crematorium as a funeral venue for all sorts of reasons. They've been before. They know the routine. When your mind is clouded with grief, this familiarity offers some comfort.

Some people think that you have to have a funeral at the crematorium because it's official. It's not. There is no such thing as an official funeral venue. You can hold a funeral anywhere.

What are crematoria like?

Older crematorium chapels are usually built like cheap Christian churches and tend to be gloomy. Newer ones have a less overtly Christian feel, but many have a cross – which you can have removed if you wish. The best are proper multi-faith spaces, have big picture windows and incorporate the landscape into the design.

Inside, the coffin is placed on a raised platform called a catafalque. In some crematoria curtains come across at the moment of farewell – the committal. In others the coffin descends. This doesn't have to happen. It's up to you.

Many crematoria still have an organ and organist. All have a music system capable of playing tapes and CDs. Some employ the Wesley music system capable of downloading from the internet just about any piece of music ever recorded. Very few are equipped for a multimedia presentation.

Increasingly, crematoria are installing cameras which can relay a funeral over the internet, via a secure link, for people who cannot make it to the funeral.

Most crematoria are owned by their local authority, but more and more are being handed over to private subcontractors, notably Dignity Funerals, one of the big nationwide conglomerates.

Prices are set or determined by the local authority not according to cost but according to how much profit they want to make out of their crematorium. That is why crematorium fees vary throughout the country. Yes, taxes don't end with death. The fee incorporates the dead person's last community charge payment.

A very few crematoria have excellent parking, clean toilets and tidy, well-kept grounds. Most skimp. There is unlikely to be anywhere to buy a coffee. It may not be possible to get there by bus. Even though crematoria and their grounds are community spaces, most feel cut off from their community.

Staff are often superb despite low wages and local councillors who stubbornly refuse to refurbish or upgrade services. Most try to look after people as best they can.

If you want to know what your local crematorium looks like, make an appointment to go and have a look. They'll show you behind the scenes, too. Give them a ring. Chances are they'll be very pleased to see you.

Drawbacks

There are disadvantages to holding a funeral at the crematorium.

The greatest of these is the short time allocated for each funeral. The norm is 30 minutes, though more and more crematoria are moving to 45 minutes. If you have a 30-minute slot, it will take you five minutes to get everyone in and five to get them out, leaving just twenty minutes for the ceremony. If you have a 45-minute slot, they'll want you out in half an hour.

Seating in the ceremony hall is usually fixed, making it impossible to arrange an intimate circle or semicircle of chairs for a small funeral. Crematoria don't do intimacy.

This system is greatly to the advantage of everyone but you. An efficient crematorium is one which cremates the most bodies possible in a day. That's why it feels like a production line. It is. A prosperous undertaker is one who conducts the most funerals. A Church of England minister can knock off a funeral service in fifteen to twenty minutes, hence the 'traditional' 30-minute slot. Thirty minutes suits crematoria, funeral directors and ministers just fine.

Hence the sausage-factory quality of most crematoria. You file in through one door and out through another. As you go out, the next lot are coming in. What ought to be a unique and very special occasion can easily become something routine, hasty, impersonal, even something of a melee.

This exposes the essential incapacity of a crematorium to fulfil its dual function as incinerator and ceremony space. An efficient incinerator hurries through as many bodies as possible around the clock. A non-dysfunctional ceremonial space gives people all the time they need. It would make more sense for bodies to be burned in a dedicated plant serving several ceremonial spaces. Given the lack of interest most people show in what happens after the curtains close, it would seem to be immaterial if a body is burned a few feet away from the ceremonial space or a few miles. Those few who do wish to see everything through and done properly could still do so. Sure, they would find themselves in an industrial environment, but scarcely more so than behind the scenes at a crematorium.

Book a double slot

If you reckon you'll need more than 30 or 45 minutes for your funeral ceremony, you can book a double slot. It will cost you less than double the fee for one slot. Your undertaker may well not tell you about this because it is not in his or her interest to tie up personnel and vehicles for longer than absolutely necessary.

Thinking outside the crematorium – other funeral venues

If you'd rather not use the crematorium chapel for your funeral ceremony you must find another venue. Remember: if it's cremation you want, this will increase your costs because a crematorium does not reduce its fee for cremation only. What's more, you will almost certainly take up more of your funeral director's time, and there will be a charge for that.

In the case of a burial, you can hold the entire ceremony at the graveside.

You can have a funeral ceremony almost anywhere. No public place is off-limits. You could all go the beach. If it's not a deserted beach you could attract unwelcome attention, of course. No one, though, could claim to be outraged and call the police. You only break the law and cause an outrage if you expose an uncovered dead body. So, if you feel like trudging with the coffin to the top of a favourite hill, do it. You may startle a few walkers on the way, but so long as you don't obstruct them, you've a perfect right to be there.

Here are some suggestions:

- Your house or garden.
- Your local pub.
- A hotel.
- A nearby stately home.
- A football stadium.
- A barn on a farm.

- A village hall.

- A cricket pavilion.

All you need to do is get the agreement of the owners of the venue to have a dead body on their premises.

You can spend time beforehand decorating your venue and arranging the furniture as you want. You can spend as much time there as you need.

You may want a venue where you can feed everyone afterwards. How then do you build the burial or cremation into the proceedings without compelling everyone to trek to the crematorium or cemetery and come all the way back again?

The answer is to have your ceremony at the venue. Afterwards, members of the family, or just a single person, can go with the coffin to the crematorium or burial ground, commit it and return.

There are as yet very few venues where you can combine a funeral ceremony, a burial and a reception. One such is Memorial Woodlands, to the north of Bristol. On one site they have a chapel, a woodland burial ground and a reception hall. They allow only one funeral a day, and people stay until they are ready to leave.

- memorialwoodlands.com.

More ideas

Time to Go by Jean Francis and published by iUniverse describes more than 30 funerals of all sorts, some alternative, some conventional, some themed, all inspiring. A great fund of ideas and inspiration for those who want to think outside the crematorium.

20

Who will lead the funeral ceremony?

Celebrants – what do they do?

How do you find a priest?

Does a celebrant have the same powers as a priest?

How important will this person be to me?

Will my undertaker be able to recommend anyone?

Where else can I look for a celebrant?

How much do they cost?

Can I plan a funeral before someone dies?

You do not need to have someone official to create and lead the funeral ceremony unless you or the person who has died wants a religious funeral, in which case you'll want a religious celebrant, a priest.

We don't go to church but we want a religious funeral. How do we find a priest?

If you are not in touch with your faith group but still want a full-on religious service, you will need to find a priest to perform it. Everyone has the right to a Church of England funeral in their own parish. But clergy numbers are falling and the Church has to rely on retired priests to cope with demand. Funerals conducted at crematoria are seen as a good source of income by some retired priests. They are known in the trade as crem cowboys. Some of them cram in as many funerals as they can, and may not do them at all well. Ask your funeral director which ones are any good. Say you will hold them accountable if you are not entirely satisfied.

Any fee you pay a priest to hold a funeral in church, however, does not go into the priest's pocket, but into church funds. The Church of England is presently drawing up rules for retired priests, requiring them to inform the diocese when they lead a funeral. In return for being brought into line they will then be able to keep most of the fee.

Do it yourself

You can create your own funeral ceremony and do it all yourself.

But creating a funeral ceremony from scratch may seem like a very daunting prospect. What's more, you may reckon that, on the day, you simply won't be up to standing in front of everybody and taking the lead because you may be overwhelmed by emotion. If that is so, you can employ a secular *celebrant* to help you create the ceremony and, if you like, lead it for you.

Celebrants

From this point on we shall talk about religious celebrants as priests, and secular celebrants as celebrants.

Even if you don't think you'll be up to speaking, you can make sure that every word spoken is yours or approved by you. A good celebrant will work with you, to your instructions, either to create, or help you create, a ceremony that is right for you. Celebrants have expertise and experience that will almost certainly be very useful to you. They know what works. Their advice is worth taking.

If you want to create a particularly elaborate funeral, or if you cannot find a funeral director who can interpret your wishes, you might like to consider employing an *event organizer* who specializes in funerals.

• Sentiment Farewells: sentiment-farewells.co.uk.

• The Fantastic Funeral Company: fantasticfunerals.co.uk. (Also plans funerals with people with life-limiting illnesses.)

What are they like?

Celebrants have evolved to meet the needs of people for whom a mainstream religious funeral would miss the point. These people want a funeral which:

• expresses their own beliefs;

• focuses on the life of the person who has died.

Celebrants tend to be middle-aged and educated. They're not in it for the money if they've got any sense, because there's little money to be made from it. Some try to, and work flat out, but it's doubtful whether it is possible to do more than three funerals a week and stay focused, let alone sane.

It's the sort of job that best suits someone who is self-employed with a portfolio career, or has retired early and wants to top up their pension. Hardly any have a funeral industry background.

Why do they do it? Many were inspired by especially bad or good funerals they have been to. They think funerals are important, and they think they have the skills required to deliver good ones.

What skills do they have?

A good funeral celebrant needs to be:

- a good listener;
- a good writer;
- a good performer.

That's a pretty rare combination.

Does a celebrant have the same powers as a priest?

A celebrant does not have the powers of a priest. Priestly powers vary from faith group to faith group. In some Christian churches, priests have the power to act *in persona Christe* – on behalf of, in the name of, Christ. This power is given to them when they are ordained.

Perhaps you do not want a full-blown religious service but you do want, say, the words of the committal (when the coffin goes into the grave or the curtains are drawn at a crematorium) to be spoken by a priest in order to give them full spiritual power. If so, you are going to need a priest to work alongside either you or a celebrant. Most priests like to run the show completely and will not settle for playing a small part. Remember, a religious funeral is not a tailor-made ceremony, it is a universal ritual which can only be personalized up to a point. Some priests, though, will be quite happy to perform just the religious bits.

How important will my celebrant be to me?

The person who works with you to create the funeral ceremony will almost certainly be more important to you, in the days between death and the funeral, than your funeral director.

The focus of attention for most funeral directors is looking after the body of the person who has died and making practical arrangements. The focus of attention for the celebrant is you: working with you to create a ceremony which will give the person who has died a memorable, meaningful send-off.

For you, the funeral arrangements reach their climax in the funeral ceremony – obviously. Remember: this is not the case for most funeral directors. Their job is to get the body to the crematorium or cemetery on time. For them, the climax of the event is the arrival of the cortege. Once there, they hand over to the priest or celebrant. They play no part in the funeral itself after they have got everyone seated, because there is no part for them to play.

How do I choose a celebrant?

Your celebrant works for *you*, not the undertaker.

Anyone can set themselves up as a funeral celebrant just like that, untrained. There are lots of celebrants out there, freelancers, all wanting your business. In theory, you can pick any one you like.

In practice, your freedom to choose has been curtailed by the undertakers and by the celebrants themselves. Bad habits have grown deep roots. Most people passively go along with whoever their funeral director says will be best for them. They allow themselves to have a celebrant assigned to them.

Here's the reason why. When making arrangements for your funeral, your funeral director needs to establish when personnel, hearse, celebrant and crematorium or burial ground will be available at the same time. This is most easily established in a series of phone calls at the same meeting. A funeral director doesn't want to wait while you go home, interview celebrants, check when they're available and plump for the one you fancy. This is administratively inconvenient and it eats time. There is also no commercial motivation. Funeral directors make plenty of money from the coffins they sell, which is why they'll give you all the time you need to browse their coffin catalogue. They make no money out of celebrants, so most of them keep no celebrant catalogue.

Clients have come to rely on funeral directors for referrals, so celebrants rely slavishly on funeral directors for referrals. That's why most don't advertise.

They suck up to funeral directors instead. Funeral directors reward them by keeping a very small stable of hand-picked celebrants, typically one favoured humanist, one favoured semi-religious celebrant and a couple of backstops in case of emergency. Enough's enough. And although celebrants are freelancers, some undertakers will never refer clients to a celebrant who 'works' for a rival.

The upshot is that celebrants aren't competing for business – a recipe for complacency. And newly qualified celebrants, however brilliant, can't find work. If Daniel Craig were to retrain as a celebrant tomorrow and offer himself to funeral directors, the response he'd most likely get is, 'Thanks, mate, I've already got one.'

And that wacky pagan celebrant with the long hair is getting no work at all because he's not old school like us; he'd frighten the hearses.

This is the way things are now. Things would improve if celebrants insisted on being chosen by their clients, not assigned to them. They won't. They've grown too idle and servile.

But you can turn the tables.

You want a celebrant who shares your values and is demonstrably good. Evidence of training and commitment to best practice and professional development may also be important to you.

Your celebrant will be your chosen representative at the funeral. In short, you are looking for 'my sort of person'.

It's worth asking around your friends and finding out if any of them has been to a well-run funeral.

funeralcelebrants.org.uk

It's also well worth your while visiting the funeralcelebrants.org.uk website, which lists every celebrant in the country. Search by postcode and make a judgement according to what celebrants say about themselves and what they look like. Draw up a shortlist.

If you do not have access to the internet, ask your funeral director to download the profiles of all local celebrants. Then take time to choose. Your funeral director will be able to give you a steer – up to a point. Good celebrants make funeral directors look good.

This website is still young and most celebrants have not yet reckoned it necessary to post full profiles. You will have to ring around and interview them. Do that. It will make all the difference.

Here's who you're looking for

Here are most of the attributes and qualities you are looking for. Tick those which are most important to you.

☐ Gender.

☐ Personality.

☐ Appearance.

☐ Training.

☐ Membership of a professional body.

☐ Accent.

☐ Social class.

☐ Education.

☐ Ethnicity.

☐ Performance style.

☐ Fee.

When you make contact with a celebrant, find out how busy they are. Those who do more than four funerals a week are probably spreading themselves too thin to be able to give you best value.

If, after you've called, you still can't decide if they're any good, ask them to give you the phone number of someone whose funeral they have led. Get a second opinion.

Questions to ask when you phone

When you phone a celebrant, be sure to ask the questions that are important to you. Take a pencil and tick the ones you want to ask.

- ☐ How many funerals do you do a week?
- ☐ Will you come and see me at home?
- ☐ Will it be easy for me to reach you to talk to during the day and in the evenings?
- ☐ Can we go on working on the funeral, making changes to it, right up to the day of the funeral?
- ☐ Will you check every word with me before the funeral?
- ☐ Will you give me a presentation copy of the script afterwards?
- ☐ I'd like to speak to one of your clients. Can you put me in touch?
- ☐ How much do you charge?

Professional bodies

There are organizations which train celebrants, hold them to a code of conduct and list them on their websites. Many of their members are very good, some indifferent.

Some of the best celebrants don't belong to any organization. The worst don't, either.

The following list is not comprehensive, but these organizations offer a high degree of reliability.

The British Humanist Association (BHA)

The British Humanist Association is the pioneer in the field of providing alternatives to religious funerals. The reputation of its Humanist Ceremonies™ network rides high; everyone speaks well of humanist celebrants. Humanist Ceremonies™ celebrants are trained and accredited by the BHA and the network extends across England and Wales. The BHA's sister organization, the Humanist Society of Scotland, also trains and runs a network of humanist celebrants. All trained and accredited celebrants in the BHA's Humanist Ceremonies™ network agree to abide by its code of conduct.

Humanists are atheists, so if you want a hymn or a prayer in the funeral, a humanist celebrant may not be for you. They will, though, include a period of silence in the ceremony where anyone who wants can say a quiet prayer. Here is what they say about themselves: 'Nothing in a humanist ceremony would offend people who may be uneasy about a non-religious funeral. The idea is not to be hostile to religious beliefs, but to focus in a sincere way on the reality of the life that has ended.' They offer a highly personal funeral ceremony.

There are also quite a few BHA-trained celebrants who are no longer members of the BHA and will allow some religious elements in the ceremony, and there are celebrants who call themselves humanists but have not been trained by the BHA.

- Find a BHA-trained humanist celebrant in England or Wales at: http://www.humanism.org.uk/ceremonies/search-for-a-celebrant.

- Find a trained humanist celebrant in Scotland by contacting the Humanist Society of Scotland here: http://www.humanism-scotland.org.uk/find-a-celebrant/search.html.

If you'd like to conduct your own humanist funeral, the BHA publishes a helpful book, *Funerals Without God*. Order it online: http://www.humanism.org.uk/shop/ceremonies.

The Institute of Civil Funerals (IoCF)

Civil Ceremonies Ltd trains *civil funeral celebrants*. They are assessed and examined and their qualification is externally accredited. Once qualified, these celebrants may join the Institute of Civil Funerals. They work with people who don't want a full-blown religious ceremony, but may want to incorporate some religious elements – a hymn, a prayer. They also work with people who want a godless funeral. A civil funeral is, in their words, 'a funeral which is driven by the wishes, beliefs and values of the deceased and their family, not by the beliefs or ideology of the person conducting the funeral'. In other words, it doesn't matter what the celebrant thinks: he or she says what *you* think.

All members of the IoCF abide by a code of conduct, are committed to continuing professional development and have their work monitored by the Institute.

There are trained civil funeral celebrants who are not members of the IoCF and there are people out there who call themselves civil celebrants who have not been trained by the IoCF.

The Association of Independent Celebrants (AOIC)

The AOIC is a rainbow coalition of celebrants who want to be members of a professional body but also want to retain their independence and individual way of doing things, and may be uncomfortable with the more rigorous, corporate membership requirements of the IoCF and BHA. Many are trained by the UK College of Celebrancy, some by other bodies. Some have no training at all but must be experienced and their quality attested to by a client or funeral director.

For this reason, there's a characterful spectrum of AOIC celebrants. There are all sorts, from pagans to ex-priests. Some are wacky, some are staid. Most are secular. All sign up to a code of ethics and a code of practice.

Here's what they say about themselves:

'Generally our members conduct funeral services for those who have no church affiliation, but some families may still want a small element of religion or spirituality included within the service such as a hymn, prayer or blessing. Celebrants will also conduct completely non-religious funerals when requested. The most important factor however is that celebrants provide families with the exact service they want and one which is specifically tailored to their personal wishes.'

• Find an AOIC celebrant at: independentcelebrants.com.

The Interfaith Seminary

The Interfaith Seminary trains people in a two-year course to 'serve the spiritual needs of people from all faiths and none'. Its ministers do not sign up to just one religion. Instead, 'the Interfaith Seminary, believing that there is One God/Truth and many paths leading to the Source of All, is grounded in a universal and inclusive approach to spirituality. It is not designed as a rival to traditional religions.'

Interfaith ministers are well suited to people who have their own, personal spiritual beliefs but have not signed up to a mainstream religion. They are also happy to conduct funerals for people who have no faith at all. They specialize in creating highly personal ceremonies and are noted for the care they take.

Find out more at: theinterfaithseminary.com. Click on their links page to see if there is an interfaith minister near you. Some are members of the AOIC.

Warning!

Some local authorities offer civil funeral celebrants. Why? Because, they say, they have a statutory duty to promote wellbeing. Mostly, their funeral celebrants are registrars, whose skills at doing weddings are reckoned to be transferable to funerals. Registrars are presently an endangered species because much of their work is being computerized.

Before engaging a local authority celebrant, check their credentials and check how much time they are allowed to spend creating your ceremony.

Local authorities are not allowed to make a profit from their civil funerals, so their celebrants often come cheap.

Green fuse

Green fuse is run by Totnes-based couple Jane Morrell and Simon Smith, authors of *We Need to Talk About the Funeral – 101 Practical Ways to Commemorate and Celebrate a Life*. Green fuse offers consultancy, funeral directing and celebrant training. Their celebrants offer the same service as the IoCF and the AOIC.

There aren't many of them, yet. But they're really good.

- Find a green fuse celebrant: greenfuse.co.uk.

How much do they cost?

Celebrants come cheap. All work for a fixed fee, but may add on mileage if they have to come far. You can contact them as many times as you want for no extra charge and they work hard to create a ceremony that is right for you.

Most celebrants reckon to spend around ten hours working on your funeral ceremony – more, often. The exceptions are some local authority celebrants, who reckon they can get away with five hours tops. That's not enough.

Reckon to pay from £100 to £250, for which you will get ten or more hours' work. The best are usually those who charge the most, of course, but there are superb celebrants out there who come cheap because they are committed to making themselves available to the less well-off. At these rates, none of them is getting rich.

Most undertakers will pay your celebrant's fee on your behalf and invoice it as a disbursement. You may prefer an alternative arrangement.

What exactly do they do?

Kate calls herself a family funeral celebrant. She doesn't advertise. All the funeral directors in her area know her, and she gets all the work she can cope with from them. Why does she do this work? 'Because I believe in better funerals. Because it is so rewarding and worthwhile. How many other people can say that? And I can fit it in around my other freelance work as a painter and illustrator.'

Here she describes what she does.

> I rarely drive out to see a new family with any clear idea of who I'm going to meet. The funeral arranger e-mails all the information I need but seldom any of the information I want, like how they are coping, what sort of people they are and what kind of funeral they want. It's only the small-scale funeral director in a nearby village who seems to have time to take a real human interest in his clients. The bigger the funeral director, I find, the more of a hurry they're in.
>
> I always say yes to a cup of tea when I get there because it gives everyone a chance to get used to me being there. I always dress down so as not to

come over as intimidating. I want to get alongside these people, not keep a professional distance. Whatever they want, that's what I want for them.

Getting started is the hardest part. I don't say I'm sorry in so many words. How can I feel sorry? I don't know them. By the end of our chat I will, that's for sure. I usually break the ice by asking, 'How has today been?' and we talk about all those things you have to do when someone dies, and how the phone never stops ringing.

Most people have very little idea of how they want the funeral to be and I know they're looking to me for guidance. Many people, at first, want me to take everything off their hands, but I want them to get as involved as they can and take ownership of the funeral – make it theirs. Most people dread the prospect of planning a funeral, but once they've got the bit between their teeth I find there's usually no holding them.

I explain that we won't make any decisions at all in this first meeting; we are just going to chat. We will probably, actually, make all sorts of decisions, but I don't want them to feel burdened by responsibility, up against a deadline. There's always more time than people think.

We talk about music. And poems and readings. Do they want candles? A big photo of the person who has died? Their old hat on the coffin? Do they want the curtains to close at the end, or stay open? Who wants to speak?

When they realize how much scope they have, they really start warming to the task. Often they want me to talk about the person who has died. I always suggest that this is something they may want to write themselves, but very often they want me to do it for them. I think of this as composing a 'portrait' in words, not dissimilar to the portraits I create in paint. It's all about capturing the essence of someone's character. This word portrait celebrates the life of the person who has died, and it is incredibly important to get it right. You've got to be a good listener.

I go home and write the funeral from beginning to end. If I have been given permission, I phone up other family members and friends so that I can be sure that I am making an accurate portrait. So far as I can, I use their words. When I have finished, I either e-mail the script or take it over and discuss it with them. Now they can see for themselves the form the ceremony is going to take, and this is when they start to really take ownership of it. I encourage this. I want this funeral to go on developing until it is absolutely right. I want it to be a family affair. And, busy as people are at a time like this, I want them to see that this may be a lot more important than lots of the paperwork they have to do, much of which can wait a little longer.

By now, we probably know each other very well. Every family is different; some are more stand-offish or private. Each to their own, I say; my role is to do what they want. The ceremony script may go through several drafts, and we usually speak every day, sometimes several times. The harder I have to work, the better and more meaningful the final result.

I can get very close to some of the people I work with and, yes, the emotion can be very catching. On the day of the funeral I often feel for them very strongly indeed. I don't mind them knowing this, but I don't let it stand in the way of what I have to do. I have work to do, simple as that. Having said that, I still struggle with the idea of standing up in front of people and telling them all about somebody I have never met – but at least I am audible. And of course it's not me speaking as me: I am simply their conduit. My words are their words.

After the funeral, the nicest thing people say is, 'Do you know, Kate, I didn't think I'd ever hear myself say this, but I really enjoyed that!' A funeral is always going to be sad, but there is no reason why it shouldn't be beautiful, too.

It can be a very close relationship for a few days but, once we have given their loved one a wonderful send-off, it's a funny thing, but it's over. I have played my part.

Is it a good idea to find a celebrant before I look for an undertaker?

There is a great deal to be said for finding a celebrant before you start looking for an undertaker because it can be very difficult to make good decisions when someone has just died. Most celebrants will be pleased to offer you clear, unbiased advice, guide you through the business of, first, identifying, then negotiating with, a good undertaker and even go to the undertaker with you, if you like. This will cost you money, of course, which you may well recoup by not buying more than you need. More important than anything, you will feel in charge of the process.

Always remember this: most undertakers will tell you that you can have anything you want, but they won't tell you what you *can* have – they don't like to make bother for themselves. A good celebrant will tell you what you can have and make sure you get it.

Can I plan a funeral before someone dies? Before I die?

A celebrant will be pleased to come and see you before you or someone else dies. Highly recommended.

If you have a life-limiting illness, or simply want to plan your own funeral, it is a good idea to have the support and agreement of those who will take over where you leave off, so be sure to have your next-of-kin or a good friend with you when you make your plans. See Chapter 44/

21

A life-centred funeral

Making sense of loss.

Starting with a clean sheet

Before you start to create your funeral ceremony, you need to understand both the size of the task ahead of you and the scope of the opportunity.

For the religious minority, a funeral makes sense of death in terms of a shared belief system based in faith. When a religious person dies, everyone knows exactly what to do. The funerary rituals are familiar and time honoured. Everything follows as a matter of authority and custom. Making sense of death is religion's Unique Selling Point.

You have got nothing like this to fall back on. By rejecting a mainstream religious funeral you have to start with a clean sheet. You have to reinvent the funeral.

Making sense of loss

You may wish the funeral you create to make some sort of sense of what has happened in your own terms.

A religious funeral makes sense of life on Earth by proclaiming that it has a purpose which transcends earthly existence. It makes sense of death by proclaiming the comforting certainty that the person who has died has gone to a far, far better place. Religious people look forward to death as a gateway to unimaginable happiness. (That does not mean that they look forward to dying; that's entirely different.)

Ninety per cent of people in the UK are not active members of a faith group. At one end of the scale there are doctrinaire atheists, a minority. At the opposite end of the scale is another minority: those who have developed a personal creed which incorporates belief in an afterlife of some sort. And in the middle lie the majority, the undecideds: all those who die with an open mind, wondering more or less hopefully if they will be reunited in some non-specific destination with people they love who have gone before them. They are content to find out when and if they get there. They suppose that, if there is a judgemental deity, a good life will be rewarded.

If the funeral you create cannot look forwards and contemplate with absolute certainty the person who has died enjoying a blissfest in eternity, how are you going to make sense of your loss? What *can* you do?

A life-centred funeral

The answer is that the funeral can look backwards – *and* forwards.

The alternative to a mainstream religious funeral is a reflective ceremony which looks back over the life lived and records and celebrates everything about that person which has not been lost: their memory, their values and their example, all of which live on. If non-religious people are to derive any comfort from a funeral, it must be in the consideration of how they can look forward to their own lives continuing to be enriched by the person who has died. Much as they miss them, they would far rather they had been a part of their lives than not. This is a good pain they are feeling.

A ceremony like this can do exactly what people want a funeral to do: focus on the life of the person who has died and give thanks for that life. It can incorporate that person's wishes, beliefs and values, and those of their family and close friends, so it is much more personal than a religious ceremony, which puts God first and which has a fixed format to which you can contribute very little.

Better still, you, the organizer, have complete control over what happens.

But remember: happy memories and fond feelings do not themselves necessarily help us to make sense of death. They may serve to remind us only of how sharply we miss the person who has died. People who have not adopted or evolved a belief system which explains death have to make sense of it in their own way. That is their responsibility, not yours.

22

Do it your way

A good funeral ceremony is as unique as the life lived.

A funeral is for family and friends.

A real funeral doesn't care what anyone thinks of it.

There's only one right way

Everyone is different. For this reason, all funeral ceremonies ought to be different.

All funerals are sad, some sadder than others. People's responses to death, and the feelings they bring to the funeral, differ according to the circumstances.

When someone dies peacefully in extreme old age, those who come to the funeral may well be feeling that what has happened is in the order of things: 'He had a good innings, a good life. In the last few years his mobility hasn't been great and he's been getting very forgetful. Really, he'd had enough. Nothing could be more natural than his leaving us.' There is much to give thanks for, much to look back on with pleasure. Sadness is softened by a feeling that all is for the best.

When someone dies young, people feel angry, shocked and cheated. When they come to the funeral, these feelings will still be very raw.

When someone dies suddenly or violently, it is possible that the funeral will happen too soon for people to have been able to begin to deal with their emotions. They may be in denial or shocked disbelief.

All lives are different. People's responses to death differ, also, according to their own ideas of life and death and their feelings for the dead person. Some people are more lovable than others. Some people are funny, some are glum. Some people live rich, busy lives; others go to work, come home and watch telly.

The lives of all are measured by what they mean to those who love them.

A good funeral ceremony will be as unique as the life lived.

Keeping it real

A funeral thrives on the participation of people close to the person who has died and *may* be diminished by the participation or attendance of anyone who wasn't. For that reason, you can, if you want, invite only selected people to come.

A funeral is one of those rare events which is not necessarily improved by professionals. You can employ a professional celebrant to conduct the funeral, but remember – however brilliant your celebrant is with words, both writing them and speaking them, the validity of what he or she says will be diminished by this vitally important fact: *everyone present will know that the celebrant did not know the person who has died.* They would possibly far rather hear something less well spoken from someone who did.

A funeral is no good if it's too good. It is actually improved by wonkiness and the odd whoopsy moment. These are the things that make it real. You can get the undertaker's bearers to carry the coffin and they'll do it faultlessly; or you can get family members to carry it and it'll all be a bit nailbiting, and all the better for that. You can have an Oscar-winning actor read a Shakespeare sonnet or you can have nine-year-old Oscar read out that poem he wrote about Granddad. Oscar will trump the Oscar-winner every time.

The reason for this is that every family does things its own way. A funeral needs to be created and conducted according to the *culture, customs and language of your family.* This is no time to tidy away everything about you that makes you what you are and pretend you're just like everyone else. The eyes of the world are not on you.

A funeral is a time when the people who knew and loved the person who has died close ranks, regroup and support each other. This is a private time, a deeply personal affair. It is no one else's business.

This is why, when it comes to funerals, home cooking trumps the best chefs every time.

A real funeral couldn't care less what anybody thinks of it.

23

Can a funeral be fun?

Does humour have any part to play in a funeral?

Is it the job of a funeral to comfort the mourners?

The reinvention of the funeral has led to the rejection of the word 'funeral', which is reckoned to be tainted with misery and gloom. Many people don't want funerals any more, they want celebrations of life, and celebrations of life must of course be filled with laughter.

All sorts of glum-faced conventions have been torn up. Mourners are told to wear colourful clothes, happy music is played, funny songs sung and jokes cracked.

Some people think that things have gone too far, and they may have a point.

Is laughter grief therapy?

It is an understandable thing to laugh at death in order to show we're not afraid of it.

What's more, if people cry at weddings, there is no reason why they should not laugh at funerals. An account of someone's life will almost certainly contain funny episodes, and good, happy memories will always make us smile.

Humour has an important part to play in helping us to cope with pain. At the same time, it is important to recognize that it is not the job of a funeral to jolly people along and cheer them up. It is their responsibility to do that for themselves: to work through their grief at their own pace in their own way.

People need to grieve. Sparing their feelings can make things worse: grief denied is grief delayed. As the arranger of the funeral, your duty is to give them that opportunity. A funeral is for and about the person who has died, yes, but it is also for everyone who knew that person, too.

Let the laughter bubble up

Any death is exactly as sad as it is, and there is nothing you can do to make it otherwise.

Humour has its part to play in a funeral, but not as a cover-up for sadness. Jokes cannot displace sadness or paper over it.

Real humour is different. It bubbles up through stories about the life of the person who has died. Real humour not only makes people laugh but also points up the poignancy of the occasion. If you want to see real humour at work, listen to John Cleese's tribute to Graham Chapman on YouTube.

No one wants to create a funeral ceremony that makes a sad event sadder. But it is probably a big mistake to celebrate life without, first, having acknowledged the sadness that everyone feels.

You can't change the way things are

Some funerals will not respond to humour at all simply because everyone is still too sad – and angry, perhaps. The funeral of a baby, for example, or someone who has died too young; the funeral of someone who has committed suicide or been murdered or died of a drugs overdose. You can't get round some deaths by playing 'Always Look on the Bright Side of Life'. As more than one wise person has observed, the only way round grief is through it. They may be right.

If a funeral is not emotionally truthful, it misses the point and even messes people up. You can't change the way things are by getting people to turn up in jeans and football shirts. If people are hurting, you need to address that.

Don't evade it, and don't trivialize it.

Is it the job of a funeral to comfort the mourners?

People do not go to funerals looking for comfort. Ask them. They'll tell you they are not there for themselves, they're there for the person who has died: to pay their respects, to say goodbye. They're there to support the family of the dead person, too. Making the effort to go is the last physical thing they can do for the person who has died. Going to a funeral is an entirely unselfish act.

As the arranger of the funeral, you will meet the expectations of the other mourners only if your sole focus is theirs: giving the person who has died the best possible send-off.

A good funeral will almost certainly help people to come to terms with what has happened and manage their grief. It will also offer them the chance to come together and comfort each other. But it is most important to understand that it is not your purpose to offer comfort. Comfort there will be, plenty of it, but as a by-product, and a by-product only, of the funeral, with this important proviso: only if it is any good; only if it is emotionally honest.

So: do the best job you can for the person who has died, and everyone will take great comfort from that.

24

Set your goals

Make sure you do what you need to do.

A funeral ceremony has most or all of the following goals. Tick the statements you agree with, then you will know exactly what you want to achieve.

The funeral must:

- ☐ mark the passing of this human life in a way that reflects its importance;

- ☐ create an appropriate sense of occasion;

- ☐ be a precious gift to the person who has died, the last physical thing we can do for them;

- ☐ express any spiritual views of the person who has died;

- ☐ enable family, friends and neighbours who were not present at the death to pay their respects and say goodbye. The opportunity to make the effort to come means a lot to them;

- ☐ enable them to come face to face with the finality of what has happened. The presence of the body will assist this;

- ☐ enable the communities of family, friends, work colleagues and neighbours to come together and stand by each other;

- ☐ enable these communities to begin to reconfigure themselves: to regroup and repair the gap left by the person who has died;

- ☐ confront the great mystery of death and try to make some sort of sense of it;

- ☐ acknowledge that, inevitably, people will be thinking of others they have known who have died. They need to be made to feel comfortable about this;

- ☐ reflect how everyone feels about the death and speak for their feelings, especially their sorrow;

- ☐ enable people to play a part – remembering always that their presence is participation;

- ☐ enable everyone to express their feelings;

- ☐ enable them to have their say;

- ☐ enable and encourage people to comfort each other, to give and to share strength;

- ☐ talk about the person who has died – talk *to* them if they like – and say what needs to be said, take stock of what he or she means to others and, more important, will go on meaning to them;

- ☐ consider how the work and the values of the person who has died can be carried forward by those who are left;

- ☐ celebrate life, and in particular the life of the person who has died;

- ☐ talk honestly about the person who has died – because no one is perfect;

- ☐ fix memories and feelings and establish that they live on. If the person who has died was very old, or had passed through a period of dementia, to remember them as they were in their prime;

- ☐ say 'Thank you' to the person who has died;

- ☐ let the person who has died go with dignity, love and peace;

- ☐ invite everyone to refreshments afterwards;

- ☐ ask them to make a donation to charity in remembrance.

When you come to create the funeral ceremony, make sure that it meets, at some stage, the needs of all the statements you have ticked. Some, obviously, are more important than others – but you don't want to leave anything out, do you?

25

Choose your ingredients

Words.

Music.

Silence.

Ritual.

And much more.

A funeral ceremony is a public performance. It must, therefore, contain ingredients that will enable it to engage and hold the attention of the audience.

You will notice that all the following ingredients form part of most religious worship. Religions have a long experience in staging events which appeal to the head, the heart and the senses.

The trick is to get the proportions of ingredients right. A celebrant can be an invaluable consultant in helping you to do this. Celebrants know what works and what doesn't.

The image of the cairn

A memorial cairn is a pile of stones, conical in shape. It may be made by one person or by many.

The Revd Roy Phillips advances the idea that one of the purposes of a funeral or a memorial service is 'to place a cairn at the end of one human being's journey'. This memorial cairn, he said, 'is made up of the memories, the thoughts, the feelings of all who are gathered in the one place together'. (From *Dealing Creatively With Death: A Manual of Death Education and Simple Burial*, by Ernest Morgan.)

This is a useful image. You can think of creating a funeral as building a cairn, and of each ingredient as one of the stones.

Build your cairn

In order to create an appropriate sense of occasion and hold the attention of the audience, you will need to choose from the following. Tick the ones you think you like the look of now. You'll get a chance to make firm decisions at the end.

☐ A procession.

☐ Different speakers.

☐ Everyone joining hands.

☐ Silent reflection.

☐ Music.

☐ Poetry.

☐ Prayers.

☐ Displays of photos.

☐ A multimedia presentation.

☐ Mementoes.

☐ Decoration of the venue.

☐ Candles.

☐ Flowers.

☐ Smells – incense, essential oils.

☐ Individual stems of flowers that people can put on the coffin.

☐ Funeral favours.

☐ Food.

☐ Dress code.

Who is going to speak?

Many funerals are conducted entirely by a priest or celebrant, who writes or co-writes the script and speaks every word of it. There are two reasons for this practice. First, most people do not feel confident that they will be able to create and script a funeral ceremony and, second, they don't feel they'll be able to stand up and deliver it; they think that emotion will overcome them on the day. Better, therefore, to get an outsider in who is emotionally detached.

It can be boring to have to listen to one person talking all the way through and, as we have seen earlier, it may be unsatisfactory to have a stranger take the lead at what is a private and personal event.

If you talk yourself out of being able to talk at the funeral, you definitely won't be able to. If, on the other hand, you see it as a powerful duty to the person who's died, you may get the strength from somewhere. You will, after all, be among friends willing you on. You couldn't ask for a more supportive and sympathetic audience than them. Who would you rather have a difficult emotional time in front of?

If you do not think that you will be able to lead the ceremony or speak at length, then try to introduce the celebrant yourself. To everyone else the celebrant is a stranger – the only stranger in the building. By introducing the celebrant, you give him or her legitimacy and establish that this person is your representative; that their words are your words.

As a rule of thumb, the more people you can persuade to speak, the better.

And don't overlook children: they are likely to be more fearless than adults.

Joining hands

When Christian churches first asked worshippers to exchange a sign of peace by shaking the hands of those within arm's reach, the response was one of shrivelled embarrassment. The British don't do tactile. Over time, though, it has caught on, and people now really value it.

It can produce a great sense of togetherness and solidarity when everyone at a funeral ceremony joins hands.

Silent reflection

Silence gives everyone a chance to think their own thoughts and muse on their own feelings and memories. If you are having a non-religious ceremony, here is an opportunity for religious people to say a little silent prayer of their own.

Prayers

If the person who has died had any spiritual views, you may like to offer up prayers which connect with those views.

If the person who died was spiritually neutral, you might like to include some prayers to satisfy those of the mourners who are religious.

If the person who died was an atheist, it will probably be best to leave religious mourners to say their own prayers. A good opportunity is during a silence or while a piece of music is playing.

Choose some music

The music you choose should express how you and everyone else feel. It should, of course, have a strong connection to the person who has died and is likely to include some of that person's favourites.

It is a grave mistake to play music to cheer people up. This is quite different from choosing music which, however funny or anarchic, expresses the spirit of the person who has died and the spirit of the occasion. Such a piece of music may well cheer people up!

It is also a mistake to have too much music or to expect people to sit and listen to long pieces of music. Something at the beginning, something at the end and perhaps a piece in the middle, lasting three minutes at most, will probably be quite enough for a half-hour ceremony. Seven minutes of a rock anthem, be warned, may feel, to the audience, like the wrong sort of eternity. If you want people to be able to listen to the music the dead person loved best, include a playlist in the order of service and they can do it at home, or share it on Spotify:

*   www.spotify.com.

Music can be much more powerful and evocative than spoken words – and the words of a song far less meaningful than its tune and the way it is sung. 'Goodbye My Lover' is often chosen by a mother for her dead son. The sense of the lyric does not in any way fit the occasion, but the sentiment of it does, exactly.

If you want to play recorded music, most crematoria will insist on original, not burned, CDs. Many crematoria now have the Wesley music system, which can download from the internet almost anything ever recorded. If you've forgotten the title but can hum a snatch of the tune down the phone to them, chances are they'll recognize it.

Live music works well, of course, and there are professional musicians out there of all sorts to play for you. Remember, though: a grandchild playing a recorder squawkily is likely to be far more touching than a stranger playing a harp like an angel.

If you want the funeral to move from sadness to a more celebratory or a lighter mood, choose your entry and exit music accordingly.

Choose the right music and not too much of it: that's the trick.

Find some poetry

Poetry has meaning far beyond words. People love it. Poetry speaks to the emotions and the senses. It speaks of mystery and the indefinable. It's not what a poem says that matters most, it's how it makes people feel.

This is why poetry works well in a funeral ceremony. And it provides a useful antidote to all that prose which everyone else has been speaking.

If you can't lay your hands on a good poem immediately, there are lots close by.

*   Type 'funeral poem' into your search engine and you'll be spoiled for choice.

*   Buy a copy of *Poems and Readings for Funerals* edited by Julia Watson, published by Penguin.

*   Buy *Seasons of Life: Prose and Poetry for Secular Ceremonies and Private Reflection*, published by the Rationalist Press.

*   Buy *The Complete Book of Funeral Planning, Readings and Music*, published by Foulsham.

Perhaps a member of your family or a close friend would like to write a special poem. Even if you don't think it's very good, it is likely to go down better than a 'real' one.

Sing a song

Bringing people to their feet to sing a song joins everyone together and enables them to play a part in the funeral.

There are very few 'traditional' songs for non-religious funerals and, for this reason, favourite hymns are still popular. People don't sing them for the words, they sing them because they have been singing them all their lives: they like the tunes. 'Abide With Me' is still a funeral favourite, and 'The Lord's My Shepherd'. They seem somehow appropriate. Any religious people at the funeral will, of course, welcome this chance to voice their beliefs, so hymns serve a double purpose.

However, all sorts of secular songs are suitable too – especially songs from shows: 'You'll Never Walk Alone', 'Somewhere Over the Rainbow'. Most pop songs do not lend themselves to community singing, so make sure that whatever you like the sound of is singable by lots of people at the same time. James Blunt's 'You're Beautiful', for example, almost certainly wouldn't work.

Gladden the eye

If your funeral venue is a crematorium, it is good to claim this institutional space and make it yours for the time you are there.

You make the space yours by playing your own music in it. You can also do it by displaying photos or, better still, one big photo of the person who has died, and placing it beside the coffin. A closed coffin depersonalizes the person inside it; a photo alongside reassures everyone that the owner is in residence.

Lots of photos on and around the coffin work well.

So do mementoes. You can personalize the coffin with a favourite garment of the person who has died. A hat works well. So does a rug or a throw. You could lay a favourite coat over it.

You can display around the coffin emblems of the person who has died. Golf clubs. Motorcycle boots. A gardening tool. Pots of jam.

You can decorate the venue more extensively, of course, with drapes, banners or whatever. If, however, you want to have your funeral ceremony at the crematorium, you will need time to set up, and then time to take it all down and out. Your best bet, in such a case, will be to book a double slot.

Flowers

Flowers have always featured at funerals. They are fresh and beautiful and, in the old days, were helpful in overcoming smells from the coffin.

Florists will supply all manner of 'floral tributes' in all shapes and sizes, from a coffin spray to the dead person's name spelled out in flowery letters. Many will ingeniously make a horse's head in flowers for a keen gambler, a pint of Guinness for a drinker, a pipe for a smoker and, for a football fan, the badge of their team. In the West Midlands, florists are skilled at delicately spraying flowers in Aston Villa magenta.

Flowers are declining in popularity because many see them as a waste of money. In the case of a cremation, that is arguably the case. You enjoy them for a few minutes then leave them behind. They are laid outside the following day and chucked in a skip a few days after that.

There is often an environmental cost, too – all that wire and oasis and cellophane.

A coffin spray lends beauty to the coffin which, otherwise, might look forbidding and unapproachable. It depends on the coffin and it depends on you. A willow coffin can have many flowers woven into it, top and sides. A minimalist approach would be to have just a single stem on top of the coffin. There is drama and beauty in that. A home-made arrangement is likely to be far more touching than a professional, pro-duction-line floral tribute picked from a catalogue.

After the funeral you can take the flowers home. Or you can donate them to a hospice or nursing home. The problem here is that flower arrangements take time to decon-struct – too much time. And MUM spelt out in flowery letters has blooms shorn of stems and is therefore useless.

In the case of a burial, flowers find a fitting and entirely satisfactory destination on top of the grave. Consider removing cellophane; it makes flowers swelter.

Instead of flowers, people often ask mourners for a donation to a favourite charity. Most people give far less to charity than they would have spent on flowers.

Light some candles

Candles are pleasing to the eye. Lighting them can make for a beautiful ritual and involve other mourners. This is a particularly good way of involving children.

You will need something to display candles on. A small table might do, but is likely to be a little low. A flower stand works well with a circular tray – a pizza tray – gaffer-taped to the top of it. You may have to improvise!

You could have a single candle in a candlestick surrounded by many nightlights. The central candle can symbolize love, the nightlights memories. At an early part of the ceremony, invite people to light them. At the end of the ceremony, after the farewell, they will still be burning, making the point that, though people die, love never dies and memories never die.

Some crematoria reckon candles to be a fire hazard. If yours does, demand to see their risk assessment and speak to the fire officer. The purpose of a risk assessment is to enable something to happen safely. Some crematoria allow it, so all ought to. You may need to negotiate with remorseless diplomacy.

Incense

The right incense can create an ambience. Beautiful smells can evoke a sense of wonder and mystery. You can't do this at a crematorium, though; the next people may not like it.

Eat some food

Food is unlikely to add anything to a funeral ceremony and is probably best consumed afterwards at the 'do'.

But if Granddad was famous for his love of mints, well, why not invite everyone to suck one as they listen to people talking about him?

Put something on the coffin

Whether the funeral is at the crematorium or a burial ground, you can ask people to come forward at some point and put a single flower stem on the coffin, or a sprig of herb.

Funeral favours

On the whole we don't do funeral favours in the UK. But we do have wedding favours. Same idea. You can give those who come to the funeral a little keepsake to take home with them. It could be a single seed to plant in their garden. It could be a plant. It could be some little thing that belonged to the dead person and by which they will be remembered – a trowel for one person, a book for another. Little things, but full of personal meaning.

Dress up – or down

Ask people to dress in a way that will reflect and add to the sense of occasion. Ask the undertaker to do the same, if you wish. Undertakers are often very reluctant to do this, but can look absurdly out of kilter in their traditional garb in a crowd of very informally dressed people.

Things that cost money

You will notice that you can accomplish all the purposes of a funeral ceremony at almost no cost.

Money can't buy a good funeral. Only emotional honesty can do that. Throwing money at a bad funeral will amplify its faults. But money well spent, if you've got it, can certainly enhance the experience of a good one.

In addition to mints, candles, incense and flowers, you can spend as much money as you want on:

A multimedia presentation

Words target the brain, an organ in which, at many funerals, bitrate is low. Words have their purpose and, for certain tasks, no substitute. But they have their perils, too. Words are what we use to exert reasonableness and they tend to be reductive. A funeral is no time to be wholly reasonable. The heart, the senses, must also have their day.

Words can tell life stories, and so, too, can a montage of photos set to music. Put them alongside each other and you've got a marriage made in heaven.

Very few crematoria, though, have screens to display them on. Whatever your venue, you will need a screen and a laptop computer. If there are lots of people coming, you will need projection equipment and time to set it up. Check the light in your venue. Too much bright sun flooding through a plate-glass window will wipe it out.

You can commission a presentation featuring video clips and a slideshow of still photos of the person who has died to the accompaniment of music. This will call for special projection equipment, which almost all crematoria disgracefully lack. It will also need time to be made ready.

- sentiment-productions.co.uk.

You can make your own slideshow with music using Animoto. It's inexpensive. Simply upload your photos, movie clips and an MP3 file of music and it will put together a slideshow which moves to the beat of the music. It's brilliant. If you haven't got enough photos to last for the entire music track, the trick is to use some of the same photos more than once.

- www.animoto.com.

A piper

For that haunting, Highland touch.

- Type 'funeral piper' into your search engine.

- Consult your undertaker.

- Go to pipersdirect.co.uk.

A jazz band

- eurekajazz.co.uk.

Doves

Release them after the ceremony. They can symbolize the spirit of the person who has died. Source them by asking your funeral director or go to the International White Dove Society. Their website will put you in touch with doves near you.

- whitedovesociety.org.

Balloons

They serve the same symbolic purpose as doves (or any symbolic purpose you want). They are cheaper and more easily sourced.

The Red Arrows

The sky's the limit.

26

Create a sense of occasion

The final journey.

A procession.

Serenity.

The final journey

A funeral begins when you set out with the body of the person who has died on their last journey on Earth.

You do not have to go straight to the crematorium or burial ground.

You can make this final journey really special by taking a route which takes in and even pauses at favourite and meaningful places – the church where they were married, the football ground where they spent so many Saturdays, a favourite landmark, a favourite shop . . .

Travel in the hearse. You may want to talk to the person who has died as you go along. There will be room for three of you.

You may have to limit the number of following cars, depending on traffic density.

You will need to get your timings spot on and negotiate with your funeral director.

Create a sense of occasion – a procession

Nothing creates a sense of occasion like a procession. What is a procession exactly? A procession is a ceremonial way of going from A to B, usually on foot.

In a conventional funeral procession the funeral director walks the final few hundred yards in front of the hearse, which is followed by the cars – usually glossy, black limousines laid on by the funeral director – containing the chief mourners. It can look very impressive.

It is not a very long procession, though.

And most of the following cars don't reach the destination because, at a crematorium or cemetery, they break ranks to find a parking place. In the meantime, everyone else has got there first, parked and gathered outside the chapel.

There are other possibly unsatisfactory elements. Why should it be the funeral director who walks tall while those closest to the person who has died are huddled, half hidden, in a car?

If you like the idea of a procession, think about who is going to lead it and where it will start.

Where will the procession start from?

People do not want to walk uncomfortably far in procession. Go at the pace of the infirmest and travel no further than they can comfortably walk. A hundred yards is enough.

It works best if everyone walks, because then everyone can see one another and feel the togetherness.

Choose a route which is free of traffic.

You will need somewhere where people can gather, having already parked their cars – at the gates of the crematorium, perhaps. You will need to do some research. If you live in an urban area it could be tricky, but if you live in a village it could be easy enough, and very picturesque.

You will also need to think about what order people should walk in, and whether you want anyone to walk in front of the hearse.

For a walking procession, the best kind of hearse is a horsedrawn hearse or wagon, or a hand-pulled cart. Horses walk naturally at human walking pace and give the procession a timeless feel. The drawback of a motor hearse is that it seems to go exaggeratedly slowly – to make an effort, impatiently, to hold itself back.

Instead of using a hearse or other conveyance, you can carry the coffin yourself (with five others) but together you'll need to combine strength with stamina. Several or many people can take a turn.

The procession into the venue

Once the procession reaches the funeral venue, the coffin needs to be taken from the hearse and carried inside.

In a 'traditional' funeral the customary order is: first, the priest or celebrant, then the funeral director, then the coffin, then the chief mourners, then everyone else.

If you think it inappropriate for the coffin to be preceded by two relative strangers, decide on a better order – and get rid of the strangers. You won't be able to do this at a church, where you are the guest of the priest.

Think about what music you would like to be playing as you come in.

There is only one right way: your way.

Tranquillity

If you want to create a serene and tranquil sense of occasion, you may want to do without a ceremonial procession entirely.

If so, you can have the coffin brought to the venue before anyone arrives, or bring it yourself.

As people arrive they can simply come in and sit down and be contemplative. The right music will add to the mood. The ceremony can begin when everyone is ready.

This sort of atmosphere may be particularly appropriate in the case of someone who led a simple life and died at a great age.

27

Who will be the host?

Traditionally, the funeral director is the master of ceremonies on the day.

Should it be you?

Who will do what?

Funeral directors are accustomed to running the show on the day. They see it as their responsibility to make sure that the coffin gets to the catafalque on time.

Once at the venue they customarily take charge and host the event. If anything goes wrong, the buck, they reckon, stops with them.

Theirs is the active role. They call it conducting. The part played by you and your fellow mourners is passive. You stand where you're told to stand, sit where you're told to sit, and wait until you're shown out at the end.

Many people are so disempowered by grief that they appreciate being relieved of the anxiety of having to play host at the funeral. Funeral directors love it.

If, however, you wish to play the host role yourself, you will need to make this clear to your funeral director. He or she may be miffed about this, but that's not your problem.

A funeral does not need to be hosted by just one person. This is a job you can share among others.

It is essentially the same job as that performed by ushers at a wedding, with an additional processional role as the coffin is brought into the venue. You can lead the procession yourself, host the funeral, and ask others to be ushers – to marshall guests and see them seated.

It is a big responsibility on an emotion-crowded day.

Who will carry the coffin?

Funeral directors employ bearers to carry coffins. Some carry them on their shoulders; some carry them by their handles; some put them on a trolley and wheel them along. It depends on the funeral director and their health and safety policy.

Shouldering the coffin is the traditional way. It does bearers no good – it causes back and shoulder injuries. For the beginner it looks like a perilous prospect, and for this reason accidents are few. Nothing could be worse than dropping the coffin, so everyone clings tight to anything and anybody they can.

If you want to shoulder the coffin, most funeral directors will happily collaborate and show you how to do it. Some will insist on a rehearsal with an empty coffin before the day of the funeral; others will give instructions on the spot.

Carrying the coffin by its handles is very straightforward. Wheeling it along is, in most people's eyes, a cop-out, but it does allow less muscular people to play their part.

Who will see the coffin into the cremator?

Have you ever heard of anyone witnessing the coffin going into the cremator? Does the idea shock you?

Sikhs and Hindus do it as a matter of course.

At a burial we customarily watch the coffin being lowered into the earth and no one thinks that odd, so why should we find the idea of watching the coffin go into the flames odd? We stand next to the earth, but not, for some reason, the fire.

Actually, the coffin does not go into a fire. It goes into a very hot chamber lined with firebricks. It is the ambient heat that does most of the burning, so the coffin may spontaneously combust when it goes in.

Do you feel that either you, a family member, a friend or a small group of you ought to be there to see everything through so that you can testify that it was all done properly?

If you feel a sense of duty to do this, make the arrangement with the crematorium in advance, either direct or through your funeral director. The people at the crematorium will not be put out at all, and will try to keep a cremator ready for you when the funeral is over. If they are very busy they may ask you to come back later. Most crematoria can accommodate around four witnesses.

It's all over in a moment. The coffin is charged, to use the technical term, then the door of the chamber shuts and the cremation proceeds. If you want to wait till the process is complete and then take away the ashes, you can do that by special arrangement.

A virtual funeral

When Second Life citizen Christopher Whipple wanted to hold a funeral for his father Stanley, he held a virtual funeral online. Why? Because he can't get out much and most of his friends are miles away, online – so Second Life seemed to be the logical place to hold it.

Outrageous?

By holding the funeral this way, Christopher was able to receive the support and comfort of his friends, honour his father's life and reach an audience he would never have been able to reach otherwise. There were far more people at the virtual funeral than there ever would have been at a real one, and who is to say the ceremony was any less powerful for having been virtual?

At the funeral ceremony you can see real-life photos of Christopher's father taken when he was in hospital and in his coffin.

Watch it on YouTube by typing in 'v-funeral'.

28

Decision time – celebrant and ceremony

Tick the choices you have made:

Creating and leading the ceremony

- ☐ We would like a priest.
- ☐ We would like a secular celebrant.
- ☐ What sort? _____.
- ☐ We will create and deliver the whole ceremony without outside help.
- ☐ We will co-create the ceremony with the help of a celebrant and deliver it ourselves.
- ☐ We will co-create the ceremony with the help of a celebrant and get the celebrant to be master of ceremonies on the day and deliver part of it.
- ☐ We will hand over the creation and delivery of the ceremony to a celebrant.
- ☐ We will find our own celebrant.
- ☐ Ask the funeral director for suggestions.
- ☐ We want a private funeral, by invitation only.
- ☐ We want a funeral open to all who want to come.
- ☐ Who will speak? _____.

The ingredients we would like are:

- ☐ Everyone joining hands.
- ☐ Silent reflection with/without music.
- ☐ Music_____

_____

_____

_____.

☐ Poetry _____

_____.

☐ Prayers _____

_____.

☐ Display of photos.

☐ A multimedia presentation.

☐ Mementoes. Which? _____.

☐ Decoration of the venue.

☐ Candles.

☐ Bought flower arrangements.

☐ Home-made flower arrangements.

☐ Individual stems of flowers that people can put on the coffin.

☐ Smells – incense, essential oils.

☐ Funeral favours. What? _____.

☐ Food: _____.

☐ Dress code. What? _____.

The final journey

☐ We would like the hearse to travel this special route: _____.

☐ _____/_____/_____ will sit in the hearse.

☐ We will have a procession. It will start from _____.

☐ The procession will be led by _____.

☐ The coffin will be carried in a _____.

☐ When we go into the venue, the coffin will be preceded by _____.

☐ We don't want a procession into the venue. We want the coffin to be brought there before we arrive.

Hosting the funeral

☐ The coffin will be carried into the venue by _____.

☐ Seating will be supervised by _____.

☐ We would like to see the coffin into the cremator after the ceremony (probably a maximum of three or four people).

29

Construct the ceremony

How long should a funeral be?

Ceremony format.

A possible ceremony template.

How do you know when you've got it right?

A funeral ceremony needs to be written down from beginning to end. You could try doing it all just from notes, but that might be living dangerously.

By writing it all down you can keep an eye on timings. You'll want to use the time you have in the most profitable way, and to allocate more of it to some parts of the ceremony than to others. You can time your script using this measurement: 100 words = 1 minute. Remember, if you are using a crematorium chapel, the worst thing you can do is go on too long and keep the next funeral waiting.

Writing everything down also means that you can share what's been written with other people, invite their suggestions or input, and end up with something everyone agrees is just right.

If everything is written down and someone at the funeral finds they cannot carry on, somebody else can come up and take over. This is what families and friends do for each other.

Lacking confidence?

If you feel that writing a funeral ceremony is too big a task, then engage a celebrant to help you or do it for you. Not many people would have the confidence to go it alone. You do not have to hand over completely to the celebrant. You remain in charge of the process and, of course, you have the last word on all decisions. This is what celebrants like best.

How long should a funeral be?

The best way to calculate the correct length of a funeral ceremony is to write it, see how much time it takes, then use every minute of that time – anything between six minutes and six days.

Ceremony format

It is not the policy of this guide to give information which is available elsewhere. There are books which deal with funeral ceremonies in detail. They contain a wealth of good ideas and they are well worth reading.

- *We Need To Talk About the Funeral* by Simon Smith and Jane Morrell, published by Alphabet Image. Lots of good, thoughtful ideas, and beautifully illustrated.

- *Funerals Without God* by Jane Wynne Willson, published by the British Humanist Association. In addition to a fund of practical advice, this book contains complete funeral scripts. These are humanist scripts, but are easily adapted.

A possible ceremony template

Here are some guidelines you may find helpful.

You will want the funeral ceremony to have a logical structure – a beginning, a middle and an end – and a sense of forward movement.

There is no right way to structure a funeral ceremony but here is a workable template. Follow it if you like it. If you don't like it, your reaction against it may show you the way ahead.

You can intersperse these sections with songs, poems, readings, a candle ceremony and music.

1. Welcome and notices

Thank everyone for coming and tell them what that means to you. Invite them to come along to refreshments/make a donation/attend the dove release afterwards.

2. Why we are here

Tell everyone what is going to happen and why. Describe the purpose of the funeral.

3. How we feel

Deal with the really sad bit now. Talk about the death and how you all feel about it. Once you have done that, you are free to give your entire attention to the life of the person who has died and talk about nothing else. Consider concluding with a poem or reading about life and death.

4. Remembering

Tell the life story and celebrate the life. This is often called the tribute or the eulogy. It forms the big heart of the ceremony.

Recount episodes from the life of the person who has died which illuminate their virtues and uniqueness and unforgettableness.

Find some tips on writing a tribute below.

5. Farewell

This is often called the committal. It is the part of the ceremony when everyone says goodbye to the body of the person who has died. At a crematorium it is customary, at this stage, for the coffin to be hidden by curtains, or for the coffin to descend. It is, of course, an intensely emotional moment. Many people assume that, once the coffin is hidden from view, it goes straight into the cremator. It doesn't. At most crematoria it just sits there.

The coffin does not have to disappear like this. A farewell can work just as well when the coffin stays in full view. At the end of the ceremony people can come up to it, touch it, place a flower on it, and say their own last goodbye. If this is what you want, be sure to tell people in advance otherwise they might think that there's been a mistake.

If you decide you would like the coffin to disappear, and you have engaged a celebrant to lead the ceremony, do you want to push the button which operates the curtains? If not, why not?

At a crematorium the organist may ask you if you would like to have music play as the farewell words are spoken and the coffin descends. By this, he or she means a few blurry, atmospheric chords. Do you think this will be distracting or do you think it may add to the mood of the moment? Would you like to play your own recorded music? If you do, remember that everyone will probably be standing. You won't want to play it all; you'll have to fade it out. This could be unsatisfactory.

6. Closing words

Words which speak of acceptance and looking forward may, you feel, be an appropriate way to end the ceremony.

Check the script

When you have written your script, check that it

- meets the goals you set;
- has a beginning, a middle and an end, and a sense of flow;
- will enable everyone present to participate;
- doesn't exceed any time limit.

Is a funeral something you can look forward to?

It is customary to dread funerals and only to want them to be over and done with. A funeral, so the reckoning goes, has to be the ultimate forgettable event.

Hopefully, this is not now your view.

A funeral is a great occasion, a great rite of passage. It has all the elements of all the other rites of passage with the majestic addition of finality. It is arguably the greatest of them all.

You will know when you have created a really fitting funeral ceremony because that is when you will find yourself, yes, actually looking forward to it, and only wishing the dead person could be there too. If this is not how you expected to feel, it is exactly how you should.

When the funeral is over you can expect to take huge pleasure in a job well done.

It's not the done thing to take a camera to a funeral. If you want to shut your eyes tight to something, why on earth would you want to take photographs of it?

Your eyes are not shut tight. You are fully engaged. So: commemorate the funeral you have made in photographs and video.

30

Tribute-writing tips

A few guidelines on how to write a really good eulogy.

The customary way to deliver a tribute is to tell the story of someone's life from beginning to end. The problem with such a narrative is that it moves inexorably towards death. If you are celebrating the life, that's not where you want to be heading.

What's more, a life story can't include every last detail. You have to leave plenty out. So: what goes in, and in what order?

Tell them what they didn't know

The life story of the person who has died forms part of your family history. If there are young members of the family at the funeral, tell them what they don't know. A funeral is a proper time to bind the young into the continuum of your family story.

Other people at the funeral will not know the whole story. Many are unlikely to know about the early years. Tell them what's important.

Don't talk in a straight line

There is no need to tell the life story chronologically, in a series of biographical and-thens. Rather than one big story, tell a series of little ones.

A string of anecdotes which exemplify the qualities and values of the person who has died will work very well. What the person was really like is probably much more interesting than what they did.

There is no need to tell these anecdotes in the order in which they happened. Your listeners will be thoughtful and reflective. A slightly rambling narrative will suit their mood. A collage of memories works very well.

Tell the truth

No one likes to speak ill of the dead and, in truth, there are not many dead people who deserve to be badmouthed.

No one is perfect, though, and your tribute will lack emotional honesty if everyone knows that you are avoiding talking about something bad, if that bad thing was a large part of who that person was. Worse, because you're working so hard to avoid talking about it, that's all your listeners will be able to think of. In such a case it is better to confront the truth, or at least to touch on it.

Little faults and foibles are quite different. Everybody has those. They may be exasperating but they are probably also lovable. Talk about them. Talk about the things that sometimes drove you mad. You will almost certainly be met with answering, sympathetic laughter from your listeners – affectionate laughter. Some people think you shouldn't laugh at a funeral but, if someone made you laugh in life, are they going to stop just because they're dead?

Humour, when it bubbles up naturally, does not trivialize or distract from the sadness of the ceremony: on the contrary, it enhances it and lends it a very necessary emotional dimension. A funeral is an occasion where everyone is trying to keep their emotions in check. Laughter acts as an emotional safety valve.

Content is more important than delivery

A funeral is not a time when people need to hear great oratory. In fact, a brilliant public speaker may divert attention from the person he or she is talking about. A funeral is no time for egos. No one must upstage the person who has died.

For this reason, a funeral is one of those rare events when people can speak as badly as can be. So long as they can be heard, that's all that matters.

And so long as they speak from the heart and tell the truth.

Share the speaking

The purpose of a tribute is to paint a word-portrait and express what the person who has died meant and will go one meaning to everyone who knew them.

You can probably achieve this better if several people speak from their own experience. They do not have to speak for long. Just one little story can say it all.

Avoid the trap

You can think of a funeral as theatre. The star of the show is the person in the coffin. Woe betide anyone who upstages that person.

People delivering a tribute can easily fall into this trap. They talk about the dead person as someone who orbited their own life. 'This is how I felt about her; this is what she meant to me, did to me, said to me; I remember that time when I . . .'

Too much I and too much me. Audiences don't like that.

A funeral is *for* the dead person and it is *for* those who mourn. But it is *about* the dead person and the dead person only. Minor characters are allowed, of course, but in peripheral roles only.

31

Funeral food

Where will you go after the funeral?

What will you eat?

What will you drink?

Why do we do it?

In all cultures, funerals have been followed by feasting. We don't call it a funeral feast any more. In fact, we don't really know what to call it. We don't say party because that would sound too jolly. Instead, we talk about refreshments or a reception or a do or a wake. Any of these pale and insecure words will do with the exception of wake. Waking a body is spending time with it between death and the funeral. It's too late for that now.

Whatever you call it, you may want to have one. Your dead person may have wanted you to have one, too. There are, of course, caterers waiting for your call. And local pubs and hotels. Alternatively, you might like to invite everyone home. That could cost you hours of preparation. So why not ask people to bring food? You will probably find them delighted to be asked. It's very hard, when someone suffers a bereavement, to know what to say and what to do. At a time like this, your friends want to show you they care. Give them the chance.

After the emotional intensity of the funeral, the 'do' afterwards usually comes as a relief and a release. It depends on the circumstances, of course, but even the saddest funerals tend to be followed by a significant lightening up. There are other factors at work. When it comes to pulling power, only a funeral can reunite so many people – distant relatives, old friends. We gather for our dead in a way we never would if they were still alive. We gather for each other, too. At a time like this we want to be with each other.

The longer a funeral party goes on, the more it begins to resemble a wedding. There may be everything to be said for letting it go on as long as it wants.

32

Funeral directors – what are they like and what do they know?

What's in a name?

Why were they called undertakers?

What's new?

Why would anyone do it?

What are they like?

What do they know?

Do they actually care?

Do they have an image problem?

Why do they dress up like that?

Why are they usually men?

Are funeral directors really like this?

What's in a name?

Most of us still call funeral directors undertakers but in fact they rebranded as funeral directors some 70 years ago. Why? Because they are sensitive about their status. 'Funeral director' sounds better, doesn't it? More professional? More commanding?

It is not an accurate term, though. Funeral directors do all sorts of indispensable things, but very few ever direct a funeral ceremony. Their job is to make all the practical arrangements leading up to it. 'Funeral arranger' would actually be a more accurate job title. Or old-fashioned 'undertaker'. Why not?

Why were they called undertakers?

Undertakers first called themselves undertakers in the late 1600s because that's precisely what they did: they undertook to supply you with whatever you needed to arrange a funeral. A coffin. Transport to the burial ground. All the trappings of a funeral procession.

Stripped to its essentials, that's all there is to undertaking. If you want to make a living at it, you must add value to those two services, and then some.

In Victorian times, when funeral processions were very elaborate and status conscious, undertakers were able to add many services. They supplied people with all kinds of paraphernalia – cloaks, gowns, crepe, even funeral mutes to lead the procession: men dressed head to foot in black, carrying staves and wearing expressions of fathomless gloom. There were fat profits to be made, and undertakers attracted a reputation for ripping people off that has never entirely left them.

Lean times followed. Elaborate processions began to go out of fashion when the middle classes started opting for simpler funerals. Profit margins for undertakers shrank even more sharply during the First World War. At a time when soldiers were being killed in their thousands far away from their families and denied a decent funeral on home soil, it was reckoned offensive to give civilians a lavish send-off. Except in the cities, it became hard to make a living as a full-time undertaker, and the job had to be combined with another skill, often something associated with the building trade.

What's new?

Over time the undertakers' role has recovered. The big shift in their status and workload happened in the 1950s when people stopped keeping the body at home until the day of the funeral. From this time on, undertakers became, first and foremost, custodians of bodies. They added value and profit to this very basic service by doing things to bodies: refrigerating them to stop them going off; embalming them to make them look nice; displaying them in their chapels of rest looking peaceful; and transporting them on their final journey in exceedingly expensive vehicles.

When undertakers assumed complete control of dead bodies, they became powerful.

The business model

Funeral directors could never feed their families just by looking after dead bodies. They have worked hard to make themselves indispensable in other areas of funeral planning: to be a one-stop shop for all the goods and services you need – flowers, catering, service sheets, newspaper obituary, a headstone and the hire of a priest or a secular celebrant to lead the funeral ceremony. This is why they collect fees on behalf of crematoria, priests, celebrants and burial grounds, making themselves responsible for debts owed to others by their clients. This is why they hold all service and merchandize providers in dependency. Whatever money there is to be made from funerals, they've grabbed the lion's share. Thrall is all.

Call it a stranglehold if you don't like it, in which case you might go on darkly to observe that they have reinforced their position by concocting half-baked traditions in order to create an illusion of the timelessness of their calling.

It's a point of view, and it may well be unfair. After all, they must be doing a good job of meeting their clients' expectations, otherwise a new breed of better event organizer would have taken away this part of their work. It's not happened yet. But there's always a danger that it might happen. The funeral directors' business model is readily deconstructed.

Undertakers have a reputation for being highly conservative and resistant to change. It is a reputation most of them richly deserve. It is the best safeguard of their status.

What's next?

There is one crucial area of funerals over which undertakers have never gained control. The relationship between undertaker and priest is often rather like that of sergeant major and commanding officer – people from different social worlds. When the priest takes over, the undertaker stands down. As the funeral proceeds, with all its emotional intensity, the undertaker kicks his heels and talks football or sits it out in the congregation.

That alters when secular celebrants are in charge. Undertakers choose which celebrants work and how much. But they don't work in partnership with celebrants because, though the best of them can offer a high level of emotional support to their clients, the creation of a funeral ceremony is beyond the competence of most of them. It's not what they do. Undertakers tend to be practical people. Celebrants are more cerebral.

Since it is the celebrant who works with families to create what for them is the most highly valued part of the process, should it not be celebrants who are in charge, subcontracting the care of bodies to undertakers? It has been tried, but it doesn't work. People don't want the care of their dead to be subordinated in this way. Ideally, they'd like the care of the body and the creation of the ceremony to be joined up: they'd like to deal with just one practical–cerebral person.

Joined-up undertakers

There is a small but growing number of funeral directors who are both practical and cerebral. They care for bodies *and* create farewell ceremonies. Compared with mainstream undertakers, they tend to be less formal, more intelligent; less interested in appearances, more concerned with ritual.

The future may well belong to such as these. Some of them are to be found in the traditional wing, others are more radical. Here's how Rupert Callender of the Green Funeral Company describes how he and his partner Claire go about it:

> We proudly call ourselves undertakers so there is no ambiguity about what we do. When we first meet you, we are unlikely to be wearing suits. We do not have a fleet of hearses and limousines. We do not employ bearers. We do not have a standard funeral, we do not use euphemisms. We do not consider

faux-Victoriana and a mournful expression to be an assurance of respect and dignity. That is not to say we are unable to produce a traditional funeral spectacular; we have buried Generals and Lords, but we approach each funeral as unique. What is at the core of our work is honesty, acceptance and participation, even if that is just helping us to carry the coffin. In doing so, all of us become less of an audience and more of a congregation.

Now, there's a breath of fresh air!

Why would anyone do it?

Why would anyone want to be a funeral director?

If you've always supposed you'd have to be weird, warped or morbidly gloomy to be an undertaker, you'd be wrong. Weirdos may be attracted to the trade – there are some – but they don't thrive in it. Emotionally needy people are drawn to it, too – those who feed off the grief of others.

Some are born to it – those who go into the family business. Some of these may lack the zeal of their undertakerly ancestors, but they are seduced by attractive financial returns for comparatively little hard work. They can pay other people to do that.

Most of those not born into funeral directing, let's call them the vocational undertakers, are drawn to the work not because they like being around dead bodies but because they like being around living people. That really is 90 per cent of their motivation. It is important work they do, helping the living through difficult times by looking after their dead.

They probably like putting on a bit of a show, too. The dressing-up bit can be a catch.

Of course, there are those who are in it just for the money. But it is difficult to get rich quick in undertaking. It takes years to build up a business. And most Britons reckon the only good funeral is a cheap one, so margins are small.

You don't need to be an academic high-flier to become a funeral director. There are few other jobs that could make many of them feel so important.

Every day is different. There's variety. Every funeral is a drama. The hours aren't brilliant – you can be called out in the middle of the night – but, except in big cities, the work for most is not grindingly hard unless you work for one of the conglomerates, Dignity or Co-op Funeralcare. There is normally a lull in the summer and a busy patch after Christmas.

Do they actually care?

Most funeral directors can put on a good show. They can big up the empathy, switch on the sincerity, convince you they care. But what are they like when you're not looking?

Quite the reverse, some of them – those who have lost the heart for it and are simply going through the motions. It is easy to grow pompous, complacent, hardened or bored when you deal every day with clients who do not keep you on your toes, whom you can easily talk into buying the same funeral as everyone else. Busy urban funeral directors look after the bodies of all sorts of people they know nothing of and may care nothing about. Behind the scenes their indifference may turn to negligence, coarseness, disrespect. This may come as no surprise and should serve as a warning.

In rural areas it is more likely that funeral directors will know the people they are looking after. Not only that, but their private and public behaviour are much better known. They maintain their good name in the community at their commercial peril.

Having said which, there are many funeral directors who adhere to a code of behaviour whose high standards might astonish you. Behind the scenes they treat their dead bodies with immaculate courtesy. They talk to them as they wash and dress them. They knock before going into the chapel of rest. They carry coffins gently. They hold ashes' urns in both hands, never under one arm. They are exactly the same in public as in private. They have a strong sense of pride in their calling. This is the sort of funeral director you are looking for and which this guide will help you to find.

Don't expect undertakers to be grief counsellors. Why should they be? If, as a nation, we are not good at handling death, it is not their responsibility to do something about that. We hire an undertaker to take care of the practicalities, not to take away the pain. Some do offer counselling as an expression of their commitment to care. You will make your own appraisal of their qualifications for doing so.

Do they have a sense of humour?

Reassuringly, almost all undertakers and their staff are much cheerier than you might think. Remember, these are people who know what a quirky and sudden thing death is. They are reminded of it every day. They feel disturbed when someone their own age dies, just as you would be. They are deeply affected by the death of a child, just like you.

Because their work can sometimes be unpleasant – working for the coroner means stretchering out suicides, picking up long-dead derelicts from empty buildings – they tend to have an overdeveloped sense of humour. They can easily conceal their cheeriness beneath a pall of velvet sorrow. When you're not looking, their ribaldry would surprise and possibly delight you. Possibly not. Put a drink in their hands and they'll let down their hair with the best of them.

Dealing with death all day every day teaches you to keenly appreciate being alive.

Do they have an image problem?

Undertakers have an image problem, naturally – some, not all. They are the victims of popular attitudes to death. And in all cultures, those who deal with the dead are shunned to a greater or lesser extent.

Undertakers do a job which most people reckon to be unenviable – someone's got to do it – so they may be socially insecure. They know people giggle about them or dread them. They are a caste apart. Like priests, another caste, they like to attire themselves in archaic fancy dress. But whereas priests are an otherworldly caste, undertakers are ineluctably an underworldly caste. So they work hard to be thought of as respectable, professional folk, pillars of the community. And yet, while we happily shake hands with a doctor, less so with a lawyer, many of us probably wonder what's under an undertaker's fingernails. They carry round with them a little cloud of fear – you're bound to feel a frisson if someone points one out to you. Most of them are never going to be asked to open the church fête, judge a beauty pageant or open an old people's home. They like to do their bit for the community, though, and the old school sort can be relied on to sponsor bowls tournaments and charity golf days – if it gives them the chance to flog a few pre-need funeral plans.

Like policemen, they tend to join the masons and may find socializing difficult.

Some, not all.

Is it good for them, all this grief?

A funeral director's working day is awash with tears. Every day. How do they cope?

Some disengage. Andrew Leverton, the Royal Undertaker, says, 'I keep away from the emotional aspect of it . . . I try to keep things at arm's length.' Professional detachment for him means that mishaps are things like flowers being put on the wrong coffin or corteges running late. Nothing about people.

But most funeral directors find it hard not to make some kind of human connection and, once they've established some sort of rapport with their clients, they're bound to have a feeling for what's happened to them. Those who are emotionally mature can absorb the grief of others, then let it pass. This, they say, is the way the world is, and I accept that.

Does the ever-accumulating burden of misery ever get too much? The rate of emotional burn-out in the industry is low compared with vets, dentists, doctors and others in caring professions. They tend not to become drunks or suicides, and, in this bitchiest of professions, undertaker friends look out for each other.

This is how Rupert and Claire Callender of the Green Funeral Company cope: 'Engage with it, let it in, feel it and then let it out again. We don't have formal supervision, but we talk, and often cry. And sometimes we dance all night. We've not gone mad yet.'

What do they know?

In 1745 Robert Campbell, in his *The London Tradesman*, wrote this of undertakers: 'I know no one Qualification peculiarly necessary to them.' He did, though, concede that they were adept in the art of making long faces.

Were he writing today he would say the same for, astoundingly, you still need no qualifications, nor a licence of any kind, to become an undertaker. You need a licence to
operate a cattery but not a funeral home in this country. Anyone – scoundrels, incom-
petents, sex-workers, school leavers, sociopaths, stand-up comics – can open for
business tomorrow and just make it up as they go along. There are no regulatory
controls and no requirements for any occupational training. The two funeral service
trade associations, the National Association of Funeral Directors (NAFD) and the
National Society of Allied and Independent Funeral Directors (SAIF), are sensitive
about this and understandably make much of their self-regulation as embodied in
their codes of practice, the training they offer and their complaints schemes. But they
don't require training as a condition of membership, nor do they seek regulation,
though they'd be happy with a situation where all funeral directors were compelled
to be members of a trade association.

Do undertakers prey on the bereaved?

While other providers of goods and services dance to the tune of their clients, buyers
of funerals tend to be tuneless. If undertakers miss out on this vital, bracing discipline
of the market, the demanding, pernickety client, it is none of their fault. If they give
the impression that they know best, it's because they usually do.

Yes, of course they look at your postcode and work out what they reckon you can
afford. Of course they'll sell you anything they think you can pay for. At the same
time, they'll try and talk you out of buying anything they think you can't afford,
because they need you to be able to pay them.

There's a widespread public feeling that it is wrong to make money from the bereaved.
A great many undertakers would agree. The last thing most people want to buy is a
funeral.

It depends on how you look at it. If you think of a funeral as an invidious necessity,
it's going to be too expensive whatever its price.

But if you think of a funeral as a precious gift to the person who has died, you will
find that much of the merchandize and most of the service is charged at a fair commercial rate.

What price professional qualifications?

There's no academic hurdle you have to jump to become a funeral director, which is
why so many funeral directors, in their quest for respect and social standing, just love
to collect initials after their names. The vocational qualification to look for, if it matters
to you, is the Diploma in Funeral Directing. Look out for Dip. FD after the name.

Should it matter to you? Inasmuch as some of the best funeral directors do not have
a Dip. FD, no. They learnt their trade on the job. They served a good old-fashioned

apprenticeship, starting by washing cars, driving and pallbearing, and advanced through the ranks. These are practical people and they learn by doing.

The most important attribute of a funeral director is emotional intelligence, and there's no exam that can test for that.

Why do they dress up like that?

Most funeral directors revere tradition, a word we use to describe any form of behaviour for which we can advance no rational explanation beyond 'We've always done it that way.' They're a hidebound lot, and nothing defines this better than the love many of them have for Victorian fancy dress, even if their frock coats and crepe-wreathed top hats often have a costume hire quality, and despite the fact that modern funeral practices have absolutely nothing in common with the way Victorians did things. They think their clothes set them apart and make them look splendid, members of a secular priesthood. Some do decidedly look splendid. Or odd. Or absurdly anachronistic. You will have your own view.

There are aspects of the ceremonial, walking in front of the hearse, for example (paging it, they call it), which are undoubtedly magnificent if that's the sort of thing you like, but not if carried off by an unimpressive physical specimen with bad hair, flat feet and an unconvincingly arranged facial rictus. So: ten out of ten to those undertakers who rise to the occasion. We just hope they ask families first if this is what they want. Sometimes you wonder who the funeral is all about – the person who has died or the undertaker.

It's all done in the cause of dignity, for sure, dignity being that version of respect we reserve for the old, the dying and the dead. There's an element of theatre, of course. Bad funeral directors ham it up by being pompous or obsequious; good ones simply allow their behaviour to be informed by the sense of occasion and take their cue from the behaviour of the mourners.

Funeral directors and their staff who favour deep black formal attire defend it by calling it uniform. They may also be aware that, if their clothing is forbidding and even shudder-making, it's a power statement. It bigs up their mystique. This only describes their insecurity, and it would be good to see more of them with the confidence and good sense to dress approachably when they are interviewing clients. Many of the best new funeral directors dress down, recognizing the importance of levelling with people.

What else turns them on?

Because so many funeral directors are resistant to innovation, their professional lives mostly lack novelty. In any case, the care of the dead does not lend itself to technological innovation. This does not extend to vehicles. Most undertakers venerate their Lithuanian mafia-style limousines and their glossy hearses. They revere them for their own swanky sake and they polish them until they glow. They renew them whenever they can afford to. They measure their business success by the size and marque of their vehicles and exult in the envy of their fellow undertakers.

There's not necessarily much client focus here. Or is there? Most people never get the chance to ride in such magnificence. If it's all part of doing things properly, bring 'em on. If it's not your style, or if you're so grief-stricken you don't notice, it seems a bit of a waste.

How much do they earn?

Family and independent funeral directors are, if they're halfway competent, comfortably off. Vocational undertakers who work for chains of funeral directors or one of the conglomerates, Dignity or the Co-op, take home a lot less – all of them less than £25,000 a year, some a lot less than that. The profits of funerals are rarely distributed among wage slaves.

The brightest and most enterprising vocational funeral directors bravely set up on their own. Because they are motivated by a love of what they do and a desire to serve, rather than make pots of money, many of them keep their charges very low – lower than they ought.

Why are they usually men?

Funeral directors are traditionally male. Correction. Were. The women are coming, and it's a welcome sight.

When it was the custom to keep dead people at home it was women, often midwives, who laid them out, talked to the family, told them what they needed to know and offered a sympathetic shoulder to cry on. They counted for much more than the undertaker. But as more and more people died in hospital, and fewer families wanted a corpse brought home to their front room, the layers-out lost their role.

Male dominance relegated women to lesser roles. This lives on. Today, many funeral directors employ female arrangers to interview families and deal with the admin. The male funeral director may not see the family at all until the day of the funeral, and the arranger, the person you have spent all your time with, if she wants to attend the funeral, will most likely be told she can't.

The growing influence of women is tending to dissolve the focus on the material side of funerals – the limos, the top hats, the rigid formalities, the reverence for tradition. Theirs is a complementary influence and it's badly needed.

Are funeral directors really like this?

Funeral directors are not all alike and very few would agree with this description of them, which is full of generalizations. 'That's not me,' they'd say, 'though, yes, there are a heck of a lot who *are* like that.'

As in any line of work, there is a spectrum of quality. The best – and the worst – are often those who are regarded by other undertakers as 'not one of us'.

Chapter 36 will show you how to tell them apart.

33

Should funeral directors be regulated?

After all, everybody else is . . .

There are three reasons for opposing the regulation of undertakers.

First, the business of funeral directing in the UK is not, for the most part, corrupt, exploitative or incompetent. Scandals, when they happen, are more often the product of negligence than wickedness. There's no crying need for a cleanup.

Second, an undertaker doesn't do anything technical that you couldn't. It really isn't difficult to look after a dead body.

The third reason for resisting the professionalization and regulation of undertakers is this. When someone dies, it is their executor who is responsible for disposing of the body. If that's you, then you're in charge and every buck stops with you. Yes, you are the funeral director. You have to register the death. You have to apply for burial or cremation. You have to see it through. You have to demonstrate that you did. Only you can do those things, only your signature will do, and you don't have to pass any exams first.

The role of the undertaker, if you use one, is secondary, subordinate and collaborative. It is to do those things (and only those things) that you are allowed to delegate and which you don't want to do yourself. If *you* don't need a qualification, why on earth would an undertaker?

Professionalizing and regulating undertakers can only reinforce the perception that they are the default disposers of the dead and, worse, move them a step closer to being the only people allowed to do so.

You are the default disposer of your dead. The undertaker, if you choose to engage one, is your agent. That is your ancient right, and that right defines your responsibility both to yourself and to your dead.

Our dead belong to us. Let us not give them up.

Shouldn't there be more protection for the vulnerable?

A criticism often made of undertakers is that they prey on people when they are emotionally devastated and not thinking properly. This is why a funeral is often described as a distress purchase.

Most of us buy just two funerals in a lifetime. We are very inexperienced purchasers and do so only in emergency. What's more, we do very little research in advance, we don't keep an eye on the market, so we have no way of measuring value for money. We are in a market which, like any other market, bears the health warning: 'Buyer beware!' Yes, we are very vulnerable.

It is hard to see how nasty undertakers could be transformed into nice ones by government regulation. It doesn't work like that in any other industry. Undertaking is not a branch of the welfare state. And capitalism doesn't stop at death.

Where there is room for improvement – and there certainly is – it will be brought about by clients who exert informed expectations on undertakers. We have a responsibility to guard our best interests, even at a time like this. That's why you're reading this book.

If you need to complain about an undertaker

You are protected by:

- The Supply of Goods and Services Acts 1982. Check out the factsheet at berr.gov.uk.

- Both the National Association of Funeral Directors (NAFD) and The National Society of Allied & Independent Funeral Directors (SAIF) offer an arbitration service to complainants against their members. Contact details in Chapter 35.

- Check out your rights. Go to consumerdirect.gov.uk. Type 'funeral' into the searchbox.

34

Funeral directors – what do they do?

The two roles of a funeral director.

A job description.

A glimpse behind the scenes.

It may well be that the future belongs to those funeral directors who can both care for bodies and help families to identify and articulate the rituals and ceremonial which will enable them to commemorate and say goodbye to their dead in their own way.

For the time being, this is the way things presently are.

The two roles of a funeral director

Funeral directors presently have a dual role. They are:

- *Tradespeople* skilled in looking after dead bodies. They're generally good at this.

- *Event planners* who source, instruct and orchestrate service providers. As clients' expectations rise, some are finding it difficult to keep up. They cling to the old ways of doing things, certain they know best. By the time you have read this guide you will be a better event planner than most of them.

These two roles call for unrelated skills. What's more, they are easily separated.

Arranging a funeral is a fairly complex task which must be completed to a deadline and got right. There is no margin for error.

That's why most funeral directors have a control-freak side to their natures. It stems both from a terror of getting it wrong and from the fact that many of their clients are totally dependent on them. Attention to detail is vital. Nothing could be worse than arriving at the crematorium only to find that the funeral cannot go ahead because the paperwork was late. Funeral directors tend not to get it wrong. Scandals, glitches even, are few.

Military precision is what undertakers do best. They have systems. Procedures. A way of doing things, the same way every time. Foolproof. You can see how they can get to be inflexible stick-in-the-muds. It's the paranoia that keeps them up to the mark.

They reckon it takes 43 person-hours from start to finish. Here, in broad outline, is what they do:

1. Take the call announcing a death and where that death has taken place – a hospital, usually, or a hospice or a nursing home. Arrange to collect the body at a mutually convenient time. If the person has died at home or in a nursing home, the body may well have to be collected in the middle of the night. Some heavy lifting required and, possibly, difficult stairs to be negotiated.

2. Measure body for coffin.

3. See next-of-kin and make arrangements for burial or cremation – date and time. Engage a minister or celebrant. Check vehicle availability and hire in if necessary.

4. Sell ancillary services – limousines, flowers, catering, etc. Choose coffin. Order it from manufacturer.

5. Wash the body (they call it first offices) if the hospital or nursing home did not do it first (they call it last offices).

6. Embalm (optional).

7. Close eyes and mouth. Shave men. Do hair. Apply makeup.

8. Dress.

9. Put body in coffin.

10. Put it in a fridge.

11. Do paperwork – application for cremation or burial.

12. Engage pallbearers.

13. Get the music CD to the crematorium.

14. Arrange flower delivery.

15. Get the order of service to the printer.

16. Make body presentable in chapel of rest or venue of choice if family want to come and visit.

17. On the day of the funeral, screw the coffin lid down, put it in the hearse and head off to the church or crematorium. (Sometimes the coffin will go to the church the evening before.)

18. Superintend bearers or family and friends of the person who has died and ensure that the coffin is carried in safely.

19. Superintend seating.

20. Collect charitable donations.

21. Take chief mourners to wake (optional).

Who does what?

A very small-scale funeral director will do all or most of this.

In bigger funeral homes the work is divided up. An arranger does the arranging and paperwork – often part-time, almost always female. This may be the only person you meet until the day of the funeral. A mortuary assistant does the body work – prepping, they call it. Your master of ceremonies on the day of the funeral is called the conductor, and many people do not meet their conductor until he or she knocks on their door on the day of the funeral.

Bearers carry the coffin. They are almost always part-timers, and they may work for several funeral directors. A nice little earner for off-duty firefighters, ambulance drivers and retired policemen.

The bigger the operation, the greater will be the number of strangers dealing with your dead person. At a busy funeral director's, the priorities are paperwork and transport issues. The less they see of you, frankly, the happier most of them are. They need to get on.

The bigger the operation, the more impersonal it tends to be. In such an organization, the interests of the business and the interests of you, the consumer, are divergent. In balancing, on the one hand, things to do against, on the other, people to see, funeral directors have to prioritize things to do every time. They are running against the clock. You get in the way.

You do not have to engage a funeral director to be both the carer of the body of the person who has died and the event planner who will engage a celebrant, source florists and caterers and find you a venue for the funeral. If you want to plan an elaborate funeral, and you don't think there's a funeral director in your local area who can rise to the occasion, your best bet may be to engage an expert event planner.

Try it for yourself

If you enjoy online gaming and would like to discover, in a virtual sort of way, what it feels like to be a funeral director, albeit an American funeral director, you may like Funeral Quest from Robinson Technologies – rtsoft.com. The blurb promises: 'Funeral Quest is a web-based multiplayer game that simulates the world's second oldest profession – the Undertaker. You will face some mighty stiff competition however, because your adversaries will be some very alive human beings in this cutthroat game of capitalism.'

Not so very far from reality by the look of it.

35

Funeral directors – what do they cost?

Are funerals good value?

This is what you pay for.

Your itemized bill.

The professional fee.

The buried charges.

Buying time.

Parts and labour.

What is value for money?

What are disbursements?

Keeping costs to a minimum.

A simple funeral.

A simpler funeral.

The lowest-cost option.

The no-cost option.

When do you have to pay?

The trade associations NAFD and SAIF.

Are funerals good value?

Buying a funeral may not fall under the heading of pleasurable retail therapy, but then neither is replacing your roof. There is no reason why those who look after the dead should not make a reasonable living from it; most of us couldn't do without them.

Where costs have risen in recent years it has mostly been in areas outside the control of funeral directors, but for which they bill you. Cemetery and crematorium costs have risen by about 50 per cent in the past five years, but funeral directors' charges have more or less kept pace with inflation.

A significant factor in the cost of funerals is the cost of transport. Those hearses and long black limousines cost up to £90,000 each. In today's fragile environment they are beginning to look like an endangered species.

At roughly £2,400 for a cremation and £2,700 for a burial (there are regional variations), funerals aren't expensive. It depends on how you look at it. What else could you get for that price?

Whether or not funerals are good value is another matter.

This is what you pay for

You pay a funeral director for the following.

Merchandize

A coffin, an urn for ashes.

Services

Looking after the body, embalming if you wish, doing the paperwork and making arrangements for cremation or burial, hire of a hearse and other transport, use of the chapel of rest if you want to visit, and provision of bearers to carry the coffin.

Consultancy

Answering your questions, interpreting your expectations and making you aware of options across a wide range of legal, practical, social and personal issues.

Agency

Sourcing service providers – cemetery or crematorium, celebrant and other ceremony specialists, florist, caterer, printer for your order of service, someone who'll sell you a headstone. Some of these services will be in-house.

Overheads

A contribution to the costs of running the business – premises, facilities and those hideously expensive vehicles.

Disbursements

This is a silly word for bills you owe to third parties which the undertaker pays on your behalf. Why would they do that? It's all part of their drive to make themselves indispensable – and it certainly suits the third parties.

These bills include:

- Crematorium fee. Around £300–£600. Phone your local crematorium and find out.

- Cost of grave. Over £1,000 including digging and back-filling. Check with your local authority or church.

- Doctors' fees. Two × £73.50.

- Minister or celebrant. £105–£200.

- Organist. Around £50.

- Obituary announcement in newspaper – local £60–£80; national £300 per ten lines.

- Any other providers of goods and services.

You may prefer to pay these individual bills yourself. Find out. Ask yourself if, by doing so, you will be involving yourself in hassle which might distract you from more important things. It's your call.

Your itemized bill

Funeral directors are instructed by the code of practice of their trade organizations, if they are members, to display their prices prominently and present you with an itemized estimate of costs based on your first discussion with them. When the arrangements are finalized, your funeral director must give you an itemized bill showing exactly what you are paying for.

Itemized, so far as the funeral industry goes, does not necessarily mean itemized as we understand it. Most funeral directors have a pricing structure which compels them to rely on clients buying most or all of the merchandize and services they offer – in other words, a package.

The professional fee

Your funeral director will charge you a fee for professional services – i.e., for:

- expertise;

- advice;

- around 43 hours of staff time;

- overheads associated with running the business.

If you have a logical mind, you probably suppose that this professional fee varies from client to client and is calculated according to the amount of time spent on each client.

Wrong. Where most funeral directors are concerned, the professional fee is fixed. And it's not so much calculated as plucked from the air.

The professional fee ranges from around £500 to over £1,500, but if you are price-comparison shopping you are unlikely to be comparing like with like.

In the days when all funerals were pretty much the same, a price for the job seemed unobjectionable enough. But the increasing personalization of funerals is causing the funeral director's role as event organizer to grow. And the likely growth of the home funeral movement is going to cause it to shrink. How can their professional fee encompass all these?

As things stand, if you want to arrange a complex funeral which will involve the funeral director in hours of extra work, the likelihood is that he or she has no means of charging you for those extra hours. You will pay not a penny more than the un-demanding client who makes all their funeral arrangements in twenty minutes and isn't seen again until the day of the funeral.

Just in case that sounds like good value, consider this: the funeral director has no financial incentive whatever to give you any extra time you need.

And let's not overlook the fact that the undemanding client who takes up very little time inevitably subsidises those who take up lots. That client could be you.

As things are, most funeral directors cannot afford not to charge you for any services you don't want. They are used to selling package funerals, not bespoke ones. If you want to reduce your costs and, say, tell your funeral director that you will not need any bearers, and ask how much that will be off the bill, the likely reply will be that bearers are not charged separately, they are included in the professional fee.

So much for itemization. So much for transparency.

It gets worse.

The buried charges

Many funeral directors slap around 600 per cent on the price of their low- and mid-price coffins. What costs you £300 costs them about £50. Doesn't that make them look dead dodgy? In the case of bespoke or woven coffins, they charge as much as they reckon they can get away with. Are the coffin-makers happy about this?

If funeral directors banked this margin as pure profit it would, indeed, be no more than a clumsy way of mugging the bereaved. But it's not pure profit. It is part of their professional fee in disguise – because they haven't the confidence to tell you what they think they're really worth.

Yes, they keep their professional fee artificially low and they top it up – they have to – by putting the biggest mark-up they can get away with on anything they can sell you. They've got 43 hours of staff time to pay for.

Where there is no consumer scrutiny, there is no rigour. This way of charging could easily have led to greedy profiteering. All the while, though, consumers have been protected both by stiff competition between funeral directors – there are too many of them – and by their own reluctance to spend a penny more than is 'respectable' on a funeral.

Very few coffin-makers will sell to you direct for fear of being boycotted by the funeral directors. If there were no more than a respectable commercial mark-up on coffins, there would arise a booming business in online sales and much more choice than there is presently. It's coming – but it's not here yet.

Buying time

If a funeral ought to be as unique as the life lived, so should the bill. There should be a fair price for merchandize. And there should be a fair and transparent rate for the job *charged at an hourly rate* in accordance with customary business practice, made up proportionately of one-third overheads, one-third wages and one-third profit. It's not so revolutionary. This, after all, is the way you negotiate with a plumber, a lawyer, a garage or anyone else, trade or professional.

A funeral director could retort by saying that a client who wants this is like a customer who arrives at a restaurant and says, 'We've brought our own food, cutlery and chairs. We want to cook the food ourselves under the supervision of the chef. We will serve it ourselves and we'll do the washing-up afterwards. How much?'

This is not a proper analogy. In a restaurant you buy the whole package and select the food you want from the menu. It doesn't work if you meddle; it causes chaos. A meal out is not a participative event. If your experience is bad, that's your bad luck and the restaurant's fault.

If, on a scale of 0–10, 0 = doing it all yourself and 10 = asking the funeral director to do everything for you, it is the job of a funeral director to meet you wherever you are on that scale. The proper function of a funeral director is to offer you only those goods, services and advice that you ask for – because a funeral *is* a participative event. You are in charge and you decide on the size of the part you want to play. If you want to supply the coffin you've knocked up in your shed and drive your dead person to the burial ground in your SUV, that's your prerogative. Arranging a funeral is a collaborative process, even if you ask the funeral director to do everything for you. The funeral director is your partner, chosen by you.

If you choose the wrong funeral director, then, sorry, that's your bad luck and it is also your fault.

Let's look at things from a funeral director's point of view. This is James Showers of the Family Tree Funeral Company:

> There's no doubt that I dread the question from a family, 'Exactly what does your professional fee cover, given you seem to charge separately for

everything else?' Yet at the end of each funeral I know we've earned every penny of fees as well as commissions because we have absorbed the anxiety of arranging and delivering exactly what the family wanted at all times as if theirs were the easiest request in the world. The buck starts and stops and stays with us, yet we try and enable from the sidelines, wearing the huge responsibilities lightly, and remembering that we do not do 'standard' funerals. After the funeral, families feel it was worth the money. No doubt about it.

It reminds me when I was doing careful, beautiful bespoke gates and other carpentry for a living, and I could never charge enough to cover my time – knowing the client could buy an off-the-peg gate from the garden centre for a fraction of my estimated cost.

Funeral products and services are going to be un-bundled and available from hundreds of different suppliers via the internet. So we funeral directors are going to have to charge transparently for every product and service, and every hour we spend on persuading, sourcing, coaching and accompanying the family on their journey of farewell.

At Family Tree we already charge flexibly – 'guesstimating' what levels of service a particular family might require. But having done the estimate, we plunge in without regard for hourly anythings – and without feeling we have to charge for every phone call or long meeting with extended family who want to play a part. Perhaps we'll have to. But I don't want a family to feel like I do when I talk to a solicitor, knowing the meter is ticking expensively.

Either way, more demanding families will mean standing up taller for what we know from our experience will best guide, encourage and inspire. And to charge freely for this hard-won knowledge.

It's all about confidence. The best know they're worth it and, by gum, they are. This is how Eric Box of Dewsbury proclaim their charges:

As we offer a very high quality service; for many elements of our service our director's fees are higher than those of an average funeral director. Some parts of our service, such as coffins and memorials, are similar in cost to most good quality funeral directors. We do not, however, just give you an average service!

What is value for money?

A funeral is reckoned by most to be a disagreeable event. The only good one's a cheap one, people say, and if a funeral really is a low-value event, they're right.

But is it a low-value event? What's your take on this?

No one ever supposed that cheapest is necessarily best. Far from it. Low cost is not the same thing as good value, in funerals as in anything else. Simple does not necessarily equal cheap. You can gather quotes from several funeral directors, but quotes will tell you only so much. There is nothing to be said for striking a cheap deal, and funeral directors who know their worth will never haggle with you. Rightly.

So: what is a best-value funeral director?

When you eat out, do you value the food on your plate according to what you'd pay for the raw ingredients in a supermarket? No, you are happy to pay much more. Everyone is happy to pay for superb customer service.

You can't put a price on that. *That's* value for money.

And the good news is that there are some superb funeral directors out there.

Superb personal service

The measure of a good funeral director is how well they look after the dead and interact with the living. A best-value funeral director is one with whom you strike up a rapport – one who:

- can see where you're coming from;
- interprets what you want;
- won't try to up-sell you;
- opens your mind to the different ways you can do things;
- sits down and talks to you;
- explores your choices;
- tells you what that will cost, item by item;
- is available to speak to you every day;
- answers all other queries you may have;
- gives you all the time you need;
- looks after the body of the person who has died;
- directs operations on the day of the funeral if you wish.

A good funeral director is someone who doesn't do things for you but with you

Generally, very small-scale funeral directors are best placed to offer you this comprehensive personal service. Someone else may answer the phone but, crucially, you will do all your important dealings with one person. As time goes by, you will get to know each other quite well.

Don't rule out larger businesses. It all comes down to the individual funeral director on the ground, and there are some very good people out there. Whether or not they are in a position to give you all the time you need, may, though, be another matter.

Economies of scale

One of a funeral director's biggest capital outlay is on vehicles: hearse and limousines for mourners. If that funeral director does only a few funerals a week, those vehicles spend a lot of time standing idle.

An enterprising entrepreneur who buys up a cluster of local funeral homes can establish a car pool and work those vehicles to death. He or she can do exclusive deals with suppliers of goods and services and begin to enjoy significant economies of scale. The really big boys, Co-operative Funeralcare and Dignity Caring Funeral Services, even have central mortuaries where they can coffin bodies as if on a production line.

And yet the curious thing is that these outfits are among the most expensive in the industry.

Even if they were to pass on some of these economies to you in the form of lower prices, it is possible that, for reasons which we shall look at later, you wouldn't want to use them anyway.

Keeping costs to a minimum

If you have no money and are on benefits, you may be able to claim £700 towards the funeral from the Social Fund plus £1,000 for disbursements. The big snag here is that they'll only tell you after the funeral if they're willing to give you any money. Either download the explanatory leaflet at jobcentreplus.gov.uk (type 'funeral payment' into the search box) or pick one up from your Jobcentre Plus. Be warned: they make it very difficult. A funeral director will be able to help you with your application. If the person who has died has left any assets at all, they will be used to repay the money they give you.

A cheap funeral

Almost all funeral directors will offer you what they call a basic or simple funeral for around £1,000 plus disbursements – another £500 or so. Burial will cost you roughly another £700.

If you choose a simple funeral you may not be able to specify the date and time of the funeral, nor visit the person who has died. This is what the funeral director will do for you for your £1,000:

- collect the body from the place of death;

- do all the paperwork;

- look after the body;
- supply a coffin;
- provide a hearse to go direct to the nearest cemetery or crematorium;
- provide bearers;
- engage a priest or celebrant to lead the funeral ceremony.

A cheaper funeral

If you want to bring your costs down further you can try to negotiate a special rate with a funeral director for only those goods and services you cannot provide. For example, you can try to find a funeral director who will do no more than store the body. It'll cost you around £25 a day.

Take a pencil and tick only what you are completely confident you can do. Be sure that you are not going to take up the funeral director's time by phoning them up for advice. Remember: they make a living by doing things you can't.

Can you:

☐ supply your own coffin (some undertakers won't let you)?

☐ lay on your own transport?

☐ conduct the funeral service?

☐ do the paperwork?

☐ provide your own bearers to carry the coffin?

An even cheaper funeral

Your least expensive option is to leave the person who has died in the hospital mortuary, or the mortuary of the funeral director who collected them. People who die in care homes and hospices usually go straight to a funeral director's mortuary; people who die in hospital normally stay in the hospital mortuary unless there is pressure on space. If someone dies at home, some hospital mortuaries will look after them.

Make or buy a coffin. Make sure it is the right size. See the chapter on coffins.

Do all the paperwork, book the burial or cremation and pay all the fees.

On the day of the funeral, go to the mortuary of the hospital or funeral director. You will need help. Lift the body into the coffin, seal the lid and put it in whatever vehicle you have got – an estate car, perhaps, or a van. Drive to the crematorium or cemetery. Do not be late.

The hospital will not charge you for storing the body, but a funeral director will.

An alternative to this arrangement is to leave the person who has died in the hospital mortuary and have them collected, coffined and brought to the crematorium or cemetery by an undertaker on the day of the funeral. You ought to be able to negotiate a good rate for this most basic service.

A cheapest possible funeral

The cheapest way to do it is to do it all yourself, but it's not for fainthearts. See Chapter 14.

A no-cost funeral

If you are determined not to pay a penny for the funeral, then simply refuse to take responsibility for it. You will, of course, come under pressure to do so. Dig your heels in and eventually your local authority will cave in and do it all for you.

Direct cremation

If you do not wish to hold a funeral with the body present, or if you want no funeral at all, there's direct cremation (see Chapter 00).

• Simplicity Cremations: simplicitycremations.co.uk.

When do you have to pay?

It is a remarkable thing that funeral directors will offer you several thousand pounds' worth of credit with no guarantee of being paid. This is why many spend quite a lot of time chasing bad debts.

Your final bill will actually be two bills in one:

• the funeral director's bill;

• the bills the funeral director pays on your behalf – the so-called *disbursements*.

Most will not require payment of their bill before the funeral, but will offer you a discount if you do. Otherwise, payment will normally be due in 14–30 days.

Most will require you to pay disbursements before the day of the funeral.

The trade associations – NAFD and SAIF

Most funeral directors belong to one of two trade associations. Each has entry criteria and each a code of practice. Both operate a complaints procedure under the auspices of the Chartered Institute of Arbitrators. They are the National Association of Funeral Directors (NAFD) and the National Society of Allied & Independent Funeral Directors (SAIF). They inspect members' premises to make sure they are keeping up to the mark.

They confer an element of respectability on the industry. It is impressive that members pay for the privilege of being policed. Are they any guarantee of quality? No. They are a guarantee of acceptable standards, that's all.

Don't be put off if a funeral director is not a member of NAFD or SAIF.

You can see their codes of conduct on their websites:

- nafd.org.uk.
- saif.org.uk.

36

Funeral directors –
telling them apart

Four types of funeral director.

What's the difference?

Independent family funeral directors.

Chains.

The big beasts.

The minnows.

All funeral directors look pretty much the same, but the differences between the best and the worst are immense. How can you tell them apart?

Four types of undertaker

There are four types of funeral business:

1. Long-established, independent family firms.

2. Members of small- or medium-size groups of funeral directors, including regional Co-ops.

3. Members of the giant conglomerates, Dignity Caring Funerals and Co-operative Funeralcare.

4. First-generation sole traders.

What's the difference?

In 1995 the Competition Commission observed: 'Although funeral directors do compete on price, the competition is muted. The market is a long way from functioning effectively.' It went on to say, 'We also have concerns about . . . the lack of transparency of ownership of funeral directing outlets.'

Little has changed.

You will observe that very few, if any, funeral directors' advertisements differentiate them from their competitors. Seldom does one of them declare a unique selling proposition. Funeral directors think it undignified to tout for business, so they merely announce themselves. Their ads may be very dignified but they are infuriatingly uninformative.

Don't worry. We have ways of telling them apart.

What we like

In the matter of household shopping we look back with nostalgia to the high street of yesteryear. Ah, those were the days. The butcher, the baker, the grocer. In every shop a cheery greeting and great personal service. Gone. For ever. Because we bankrupted them by trooping off to the unloveable supermarket where the food is fresher, the choice greater, the prices lower. Sure, the experience is impersonal, but who cares? We can help ourselves. Bigger is better, biggest is best.

Any business which can reduce its unit price is likely to attract customers. A handbuilt car is the one we'd like, but the mass-produced car is the one we can afford.

Undertakers are an exception. We don't want a production-line funeral. We don't want to be borne to our final resting place by a supermarket chain. We don't want to deal with a faceless organization, we want to interact with humans. We want a bespoke, handbuilt, boutique funeral. Small is beautiful.

Happily, a boutique undertaker is likely to cost you less than one of the big chains.

Remember what you read in Chapter 34 about the way bigger funeral homes divide up the work? Is this an issue for you?

Let's review the four different types of funeral director available to you.

Independent family funeral directors

Do you suppose that a family funeral director is most likely to do the best job? Most people do. All the guarantees seem to be in place. They've been at it for years. They are esteemed members of your local community. They'll know what to do and they'll do it in a time-honoured way. They will give you great personal service.

There's no genetic logic to this. The skills and virtues of parents are not necessarily passed down to their children. A time-honoured way of doing things is not necessarily the best way of doing things now. And a family business of any age can get encumbered with family members who pay themselves more than they ought, preventing reinvestment.

Some family firms are some of the most stick-in-the-mud, lazy and incompetent you could find.

By sheer genetic good luck, some of them are superb. Their heritage of excellent service, their good name, mean everything to them.

The name on the sign is the name of the owner, and that person is accountable to his or her local community.

But there's nothing in a name.

Members of groups

When independent funeral directors want to sell their businesses, probably because they want to retire, they are unlikely to find someone just starting out, because no one who wants to become a funeral director has normally got that kind of money. So they have a choice: sell out to a big conglomerate, to a smaller group or to a heavily mort-gaged competitor.

As we have seen, groups of funeral homes enjoy economies of scale which make them more profitable, but they do not use this advantage to undercut their competitors. On the contrary, they may well be more expensive.

Where funerals are concerned, the normal rules of the market do not apply. A funeral home, however good, cannot stimulate an appetite for its product, neither can it inspire repeat business – it cannot encourage more people to die, nor can it encourage them to die more than once. It can only get bigger by ceaselessly devouring its rivals.

Groups know that we don't like them. Some of them are glad that we don't know that they are funded by venture capitalists. And because they can't guarantee a better service than the best independents however hard they try, they don't re-badge every business they buy and proclaim UNDER NEW MANAGEMENT.

No, the sold-out business will almost invariably go on trading under the same old name, looking for all the world as it has always done.

It's not what it seems. It's a branch. And it's run by a salaried manager. By the time you find out, it's probably too late.

Where groups are concerned, intricate, foolproof management systems usually achieve a uniform level of good practice but, of course, cannot inspire superb service. It's a bland product you may buy, safe and serviceable, lacking in character, a touch impersonal. Big operations, as you know, tend to favour personnel who are obedient conformists.

You will most likely deal with an arranger – a person, normally female, who makes your funeral arrangements with you. You may well not meet the funeral director who is to conduct your funeral until he or she knocks on your door on the day of the funeral itself.

Funeral homes which are members of groups are most likely to be characterized by harassed employees rushing to keep up. It's all about logistics. And sales targets.

There are heroic exceptions. Some branches are run superbly by employees who put the interests of their clients above their frustration with their senior managers and their poor wages. They may well do a better job than your nearest independent undertaker.

The name on the sign means nothing. The manager is accountable to head office.

There's nothing in a name.

The big beasts

The biggest conglomerates are Co-operative Funeralcare and Dignity Caring Funerals. They operate just like the smaller groups with this exception: they establish, where they can, centralized mortuaries where dead bodies go to be laid out and coffined as if on a production line. They don't necessarily tell you this. You have no idea who is handling the body of your dead person.

Dignity

Dignity is the UK's only FTSE-listed funeral director in the UK. It owns more than 540 funeral homes and conducts one in eight of all funerals in the UK. It owns 25 crematoria and cremates more than 40,000 bodies every year. With an eye on future market share, it has sold more than 350,000 'Buy now, die later' funeral plans. If you buy a funeral plan from Age Concern it is a Dignity plan. Age Concern says that Dignity guarantees a uniform level of service nationally.

Dignity is powerful. It is profitable. Its shareholders like it. The history of national funeral chains in the UK has not been a prosperous one, but Dignity, formed by a management buyout from its huge and scandal-riddled American parent, Service Corporation International, seems to be making a good fist of things.

It is in business to make money in the normal way of the market. Staff wages are held low, yet some branches offer excellent service.

Dignity funerals are some of the most expensive out there.

Its branches go on trading under the names of the original owners.

Dignity is accountable to its shareholders.

Co-operative Funeralcare

Funeralcare is a subsidiary of the Co-operative Group. It controls more than 800 funeral homes and is expanding.

The co-operative movement owes its principles to its idealistic founders, the Rochdale Pioneers, a group of working people who got together to sell food to fellow workers at affordable prices. The Rochdale Principles were a blueprint for democratic social reform.

There were once hundreds of Co-operative societies. Most have merged to form the Co-operative Group. There are still a few independent societies, some of which have adopted Co-op Group branding. Of these, a few still operate an independent funeral service. All Co-ops champion high ethical standards.

Given the economies of scale enjoyed by Funeralcare, and having in mind its foundational principles, you might expect it, as the people's undertaker, to provide the cheapest funerals out there. It doesn't.

Some branches of Funeralcare operate under that name, others under the name of their original owner. Some branches offer excellent service.

Funeralcare is accountable to Co-op Group members and its ethical principles.

The minnows

It is expensive to start up a funeral business and, given the degree of local competition, a brave thing to do.

People who start from scratch and go it alone are normally passionate about what they do. Many once worked for a conglomerate where they reacted strongly against systems of working which prevented them from giving their customers the degree of personal service they reckoned they needed. We must backhandedly bless the Co-ops, in particular, for unintentionally breeding some of our best born-again independent funeral directors.

Be aware, though, that there are some dodgy start-ups out there only in it for the money.

New businesses are normally one- or two-person affairs. They are not usually rushed off their feet, so they have more time for you. Their hearse may be an old-ish model, but perfectly serviceable. Does this matter to you? Their premises will probably not be big and well resourced, merely adequate.

Given the over-supply of funeral directors in the UK, it's pointless to start a new business if you're going to do things the way they've always been done. Some of them do, nevertheless. Yet it is in this sector that you are most likely to find progressive undertakers, often with green credentials and an un-stuffy way of going about things. Any business with 'Company' at the end of its name is likely to be one of these.

Despite their relative inefficiency, the minnows normally charge no more than anyone else – often less.

One thing you can trust: the name over the door means exactly what it says.

37

Funeral directors – find out who's out there

How to find the best funeral director near you.

Now that you know what sort of a funeral director you favour, start looking. If you live in a big town or a city, you won't have to look far. If you are out in the country, search within a radius of up to twenty miles if transport isn't an issue. You'll find someone much closer if you can, of course, but you don't want to miss any opportunities.

Where to look

Your local paper will carry adverts from funeral directors on the day they publish deaths – usually a Friday.

Use Yellow Pages.

Use the internet. Google 'funeral-director + *your nearest town*'. Very few undertakers have their own website (tells you so much about them), and those you find will probably be pretty naff.

Go to nearestfuneraldirector.co.uk. The most useful thing about this site is that it tells you who owns the business. Its only downside is that it can sometimes be slow to add in brand-new businesses.

Go to the Good Funeral Guide website, which lists best funeral directors country-wide.

Who to ask

Personal recommendation

You can seek impartial advice about good funeral directors in your area by asking around among your friends and work colleagues. It is worth taking their opinions and experiences into account. But remember: having read this book, you ought to be able to make a much more informed choice than they ever did. Remember, too, that people tend to have very low expectations of funerals and, therefore, are too easily satisfied.

Advice from care-home nurses may or may not be useful; it all depends on how well you know and trust them. Some funeral directors have ways of ingratiating themselves with carers of the elderly. It's not widespread, but it goes on.

Celebrants

Celebrants and officiants often know who's good and who's not. But because they presently depend for work on referrals from funeral directors, most would not feel comfortable to offer advice if they thought it might get back to an undertaker they had advised against. Worth a phone call, though.

The Good Funeral Guide

The Good Funeral Guide lists recommended funeral directors on its website, goodfuneralguide.co.uk

Make a shortlist

Collect around six names and phone numbers – more if you wish. It's important to get this right.

Record your choices

Now record all your funeral choices in the next chapter.

Get ready to phone

You are almost ready to start phoning funeral directors you like the look of. When you do so, you need to find out two things:

· Is this funeral director my sort of person?

· How much will they charge?

Remember, most people who call a funeral director know very little about funerals. For this reason, funeral directors are used to doing most of the talking. Because you now know so much, you will be turning the tables.

Opening questions

Here are some good opening questions. Tick the ones that are important to you:

☐ Who owns this business?

☐ How long have you been going?

☐ Why should I choose you in favour of anyone else? What makes you special?

☐ Can you guarantee that only one person will make arrangements with me, get back to me personally every time I ring, prepare the body and be the conductor on the day of the funeral?

☐ Will I be able to speak to you personally every day if I need to?

The answers to these questions will give you a flavour of the person you are dealing with. If at any stage of the conversation you get a sinking feeling, make an excuse and ring off.

Asking for a quote

If you feel like carrying on, the next thing you say is:

• I have decided on the funeral arrangements, and I would like you to give me a quote. If you'd like to make a note of them, I'll tell you what they are. I'd like you to price every item, please.

It may take an hour or two for them to do this. Request quotes from at least three funeral directors; they will enable you to negotiate. Remember: the cheapest is not necessarily the best!

38

Decision time –
buy only what you want

The complete list of choices you have made as you have read this guide.

You now have enough information to enable you to decide what you want to undertake and what you want the undertaker to undertake. It is now time to pick what you want from the undertaker's menu of goods and services.

When most people go to see an undertaker, they are asked what they want. This list will put you in the driving seat.

Make a shopping list

Take a pencil and work through this list.

Who will do the administration?

☐ _____ to complete all paperwork and pay disbursements.

☐ _____ to place an obituary notice in the paper.

Who will look after the body?

☐ The body will stay with the undertaker.

☐ The body will come home.

If you want the body to come home, how long for?

☐ For the first few days.

☐ For one/two days before the funeral.

☐ All the time.

Who will supply the coffin?

☐ I will supply the coffin (some undertakers won't let you).

☐ I have seen a coffin I like. I want the undertaker to order it.

☐ I will choose a coffin from the undertaker's range.

Who will lay out the body?

☐ I will wash and dress the body at the undertaker's.

☐ I will wash and dress the body at home with the undertaker.

☐ I will wash and dress the body at home unassisted.

☐ I want the undertaker to wash and dress the body.

If you want the undertaker to wash and dress the body, do you

☐ want someone of the same sex to do it?

Embalming and invasive treatment

☐ Yes/no to embalming, sanitary treatment or hygienic treatment.

☐ Only gentle methods to be used for closing the eyes and mouth.

What will the dead person wear?

☐ I will supply clothes for the body.

☐ The body will be clothed in a gown supplied by the undertaker.

How will the hair be groomed?

☐ I will supply a photograph of the person who has died.

☐ I will give instructions about this.

☐ The undertaker will use his or her discretion.

Do you want to visit the person who has died?

☐ No visit.

☐ One visit.

☐ One visit on the day before the funeral.

☐ As and when.

☐ Every day.

☐ Long periods.

☐ No religious imagery in the 'chapel of rest'.

Burial or cremation?

☐ Burial.

☐ If burial, where? _____.

☐ Cremation.

Funeral or direct cremation?

☐ Funeral.

☐ No funeral – straight to the crematorium.

When?

Our preferred dates and times for the funeral are:

☐ _____ morning/afternoon.

☐ _____ morning/afternoon.

☐ _____ morning/afternoon.

Where will you hold the funeral?

☐ Crematorium chapel.

☐ Cemetery chapel.

☐ Natural burial ground.

☐ Other: _____.

Who will book the funeral venue (including the crematorium)?

☐ I will book it myself and pay direct.

☐ The undertaker will do this.

How long will the ceremony last?

If it is likely to last longer than twenty minutes, you will need to book a double slot if your venue is the crematorium. Check with your crematorium how long they allow you.

☐ We'll need a single slot.

☐ We'll need a double slot.

Do you need a priest or a celebrant?

Note: you can appoint a celebrant before you have seen your undertaker. Go to funeralcelebrants.org.uk.

☐ No, we're sorted.

☐ Yes, a priest.

☐ Yes, a celebrant: semi-religious/atheist.

Do you want to witness the coffin going into the cremator?

If you do not wish to do so yourself, you may like to ask someone else to do it.

☐ No.

☐ Yes. I/the undertaker will make this arrangement.

☐ If yes, how many of you? _____.

What's the dress code?

☐ I want the undertaker and staff to wear _____.

☐ We will wear _____.

What part do you want the undertaker to play at the funeral?

☐ Master of ceremonies, in charge of everything.

☐ Record the names of the people who come.

☐ Just help out with getting people seated.

☐ No part at all. I am the host.

Arrival

☐ I want the coffin brought to the door of the crematorium chapel.

☐ I want the coffin brought to the car park, from where we will carry it ourselves.

☐ I want the coffin brought to _____ from where we will carry it ourselves.

☐ I want the coffin to be placed in the venue before we arrive _____.

What transport do you need on the day of the funeral?

☐ Undertaker's hearse.

☐ Special hearse _____.

☐ Number of following limousine/s _____.

☐ Undertaker's estate car or private ambulance.

☐ I will supply my own transport.

Procession

☐ I want the undertaker to walk in front of the hearse.

☐ I will decide who walks in front of the hearse.

Will you need bearers to carry the coffin?

☐ Yes.

☐ Yes, but only _____.

☐ No, we shall carry the coffin ourselves.

Do you want an order-of-service booklet?

☐ Yes, we want the undertaker to get it printed.

☐ Yes, we shall look after this ourselves.

☐ No, we don't one.

Who will order the flowers?

☐ I will choose from undertaker's catalogue.

☐ I will supply them.

Do you want the undertaker to collect and forward donations to a chosen charity?

☐   Yes.

☐   No.

Do you want the undertaker to supply any of the following?

☐   Catering.

☐   A piper.

☐   Live musicians.

☐   Multimedia presentation.

☐   Doves.

☐   Balloons.

☐   An urn for ashes.

Ensuring best care for the person who has died

Before you enter into a contract with your chosen funeral director, you may like your funeral director to enter into a contract with you and make a solemn undertaking to safeguard the privacy and dignity of the person who has died.

In even the better funeral homes there can be a great difference between how they behave in the front office and how they do things behind the scenes, where no one is looking. They can be high-handed.

How, for example, would you feel if your dead person had been used as the model for a training session in laying-out for visiting staff from a care home? How would you feel if you knew that your dead person had been laid out and dressed by someone while he laughed and joked with a colleague sitting in a corner of the mortuary eating his lunchtime sandwiches? How would you feel if he had been helped by a lad on work experience who went home and told his hushed mates all about it.

Commitment to best practice must be readily verifiable or it is worthless.

39

101 coffins and a shroud

Do you have to buy a coffin from an undertaker?

Can you make your own?

Who's the greenest of them all?

What else is out there?

Cardboard.

Willow.

Wool.

Cocostick and paper.

Bamboo and wild pineapple.

Jute.

Banana leaf and water hyacinth.

Ecopod.

Picture coffins.

Flat pack coffins.

Crazy coffins.

Choosing a coffin for someone is probably not a matter you have ever given much thought to, if any. When it actually comes to it, it can feel surreal.

The price you pay an undertaker for a coffin can be many times what the undertaker paid for it. This is because many undertakers 'bury' part of what they call their professional fee in the cost of their coffins. See Chapter 35.

Most undertakers sell only a limited range of coffins (so that they can negotiate keen prices with the makers). Many will not tell you what else is available, either because they can't get such a good margin on it or because they can't be bothered. If you see something here that you like the look of, tell your undertaker to get it for you. If, say, it's a wicker coffin you want, make sure your undertaker gets it from the firm which sells the one you like. There are cheap versions with a looser weave which offer your undertaker a bigger margin.

The range

Coffins these days are made from many different materials. You can have a traditional wooden one, or one made of all sorts of other materials – willow, sea grass, banana leaves, cardboard.

There's a choice of shapes, from the classic shouldered coffin to the American-style casket to the revolutionary Eco-Pod.

If you think that traditional varnished wood coffins look cold and repellent, you may be amazed by how much softer and friendlier in appearance the new-look generation is.

Most funeral directors display their limited range in a catalogue and give them posh names like The Arundel. Some have a coffin showroom.

Cost

You can spend as much as you like on a coffin, from less than £100 to several thousand pounds.

No one wants to feel like a skinflint and choose something disrespectfully cheap. But here's a thing: there's almost no difference in appearance between a bottom-of-the-range foil MDF coffin and a solid timber one at three times the price. If you throw good money at a coffin it is highly unlikely that anyone will notice unless it is made from other materials.

Given the fact that, whether it is buried or cremated, any coffin enjoys a very short life in the public eye, your choice of coffin will be influenced by three factors:

1. What you can afford.

2. Which material you think appropriate.

3. What you like the look of.

Quality and durability

Quality, so far as coffins go, is in the eye of the beholder.

For some, durability is the important thing. Durability is, of course, of no account if the coffin is to be cremated.

An American-style Batesville casket made from sixteen-gauge stainless steel with hermetic seals will, when buried, keep out water and creepy-crawlies for years. Alternatives to steel are bronze and copper. Solid timber is durable, too, especially a hardwood like mahogany.

Some people favour something ornate and magnificent. If that's you, an American-style casket may be your coffin of choice.

Anyone favouring simplicity will spurn one of these bling monsters and opt for, perhaps, a cardboard coffin or one made from wicker or pine. These, of course, are less durable when buried.

Needless to say, most funeral directors will be very happy to sell you the most expensive coffin they have – if they reckon you can afford it.

It may be that, on their least expensive coffin, there are only four handles, lending it a forlorn, cheap look designed to put you off. This may encourage you to go for something with six – but for most purposes a coffin only actually needs four.

Do you have to buy a coffin from an undertaker?

It is difficult to find coffin suppliers who will sell direct to the public. If they did, the undertakers would boycott them and try to close them down. This is one commodity you cannot yet get more cheaply on the internet. Only a consumer clamour will achieve that.

Many undertakers will not accept a coffin supplied by you (they will insist that you order it through them), though there are exceptions. All will order the coffin you want if you see something you like on the internet. Some will charge much more for it than others. Ring around, get some other quotes, and negotiate the lowest price with your undertaker.

Can you make your own?

If you want to make the coffin yourself it is most unlikely that an undertaker would refuse to use it. You will, of course, have to be able to show that it is strong enough to do its job.

Who's the greenest of them all?

Almost all coffins have passable green credentials with the notable exception of many made from MDF, which are full of chemical-crammed glues. Cardboard coffins, you might suppose, are good and green, but actually a fair amount of manufacture goes into producing the cardboard.

Of equal concern to you should be the lining of the coffin and its handles.

Perhaps the greenest coffins of all are those made from willow in the UK. The material is sustainable, the coffin-miles minimal. Yet a coffin shipped from China by Ecoffins uses, they claim, no more fuel than a car journey of 4.63 miles.

The greenest coffins in the UK are made by J. C. Atkinson, *Sunday Times* Best Green Company 2008:

- jcatkinson.co.uk.

A shroud

The greenest option of all is to do without a coffin and opt instead for a shroud. Put the body on a board and wind it in cloth. The outline of the body will be identifiable, and it is probably for this reason that, despite well-intentioned campaigning, the shroud has not made a comeback.

*   Bellacouche make beautiful felted shrouds covered in a choice of leaf patterns: bellacouche.com – Ring: 01647 432155.

What else is out there?

Here are some of the coffins a funeral director may not stock and may not offer you.

Cardboard

A cardboard coffin ought to be the cheapest you can get, you might think, but actually they are more expensive than coffins made from MDF. People who go for cardboard are really making a lifestyle statement. It is the last word in simplicity and a good choice for someone who says, 'Bury me in a binbag.' Most people would reckon it an outrageous choice, either in a good or a bad way. White or brown cardboard is good for decoration. You can paint it, draw on it, write messages on it. You can get the children to decorate their Nan's cardboard coffin – but beware: children like to use lots of red, and this can give a misleading impression. Most funeral directors now stock cardboard, but some, hating it, will cast doubt on its load-bearing capability and even its ability to withstand rain. This is nonsense. Some undertakers are able to put a cardboard coffin inside a re-usable coffin (called a coffin cover) for the funeral. An alternative is to drape the coffin with fabric of some sort – a pall.

See what a cardboard coffin looks like at:

*   greenfieldcreations.co.uk. Will sell to you direct: range starts at £81. Can carry 23 stone.
*   Do an image search. Type in 'George Melly funeral'.

Willow

Increasingly popular. You can decorate the coffin with flowers. The cheaper ones have a flimsy weave. Many willow coffins are imported; some are made in the UK. Best are:

*   Somerset Willow, woven in the Somerset Levels.
*   wickerwillowcoffins.co.uk. Will sell to you direct.
*   Mawdeseley Willow, woven in Lancashire.
*   peacefunerals.co.uk. Will sell to you direct.

Wool

Made in Yorkshire from Dorset Horn sheep's wool over a cardboard frame. Hemmed with blanket stitch.

*   naturallegacy.co.uk.

Bamboo or wild pineapple

*   ecoffins.co.uk. Will sell to you direct.

Jute

*   jfunerals.com.

Cocostick and paper

Designed and imported by Somerset Willow. Cocostick coffins are made from the stems of coconut leaves. Paper coffins are made from spun paper woven around a rigid frame.

*   naturalwovencoffins.co.uk.

Banana leaf or water hyacinth

*   daisycoffins.com.

Seagrass

*   finetimber products.co.uk. Will sell to you direct.

Ecopod

Revolutionary shape. Made from recycled paper. Come in gorgeous colours:

*   ecopod.co.uk. Will sell to you direct.

Picture coffins

Cardboard decorated with any scene or picture you like:

*   greenfieldcreations.co.uk. Will sell direct: £315.
*   colourfulcoffins.com. The same service as Greenfield but also in wood. Will not sell direct and significantly more expensive.

Flat-pack coffins

Self-assembly, plain pine:

- eco-coffins.com.

Click-to-construct coffin, ready to go in three minutes:

- everybodycoffins.com.

Crazy coffins

Bespoke coffins in all sorts of wonderful shapes

- crazycoffins.co.uk.
- eshopafrica.com.

Hand-painted coffins

- purplefunerals.com.

American caskets

- caskets.co.uk.

Bookcase coffin

Finally, if you'd like to buy your own coffin now and enjoy it till you need it, have a look at William Warren's bookcase coffin. Yes, it's a bookcase which can be reassembled as a coffin when you conk out. Go to his website, type in your size and download instructions for making it. Materials will cost around £30 for pine, more for posher woods. William, the last of the altruists, charges nothing for the download.

- williamwarren.co.uk.

40

Final rides – hearses

The right transport for that final journey.

The vehicle customarily used for transporting a dead person to his or her final resting place is the classic big black hearse.

There are, of course, alternatives, and your funeral director will know of them. If you are arranging the funeral yourself, you will find that many of the mainstream suppliers will refuse to deal with you direct.

If you think a hearse too showy and would rather have something more modest, something greener, some funeral directors will offer you an alternative – an estate car, for example, or their removal vehicle, which they use for picking up dead bodies. Many funeral directors will come over all reluctant if you do, reckoning anything less than a designated hearse to be less than 'dignified'. Put your foot down.

Most alternatives to your undertaker's hearse will be expensive. If you go ahead, be sure to make the most of it. A horse-drawn hearse, for example, makes a stunning show.

If you decide to hire a special hearse, make sure your undertaker deletes the cost of hiring his or hers. Some charge twice. There's quite enough margin for them on the hired hearse.

Variants of classic hearses

There are *vintage hearses* and limousines available nationwide. Ask your undertaker. There are *white hearses* and there are *silver hearses*. A. W. Lymn of Nottingham runs the biggest fleet of *Rolls Royces* in Europe, all of them silver. See them at: lymn.co.uk.

There is a *pink hearse*. See it at: greenscarriages.co.uk.

There is a 1974 *Cadillac hearse*. See it at: cadillachearse-hire.co.uk.

There is a *bluebell hearse*. See it at: naturalendings.co.uk.

Retro hearses

There are *retro hearses*. The most low-tech of these is a *hand bier* or *handcart*, which you would probably be best off sourcing locally. A funeral director is the person best able to help you find one.

Horsey hearses

Horse-drawn hearses are traditionally pulled by Belgian Blacks with nodding plumes of ostrich feathers. These declined in popularity after the Kray funerals, but are now as popular as ever and available throughout the UK. Timeless and marvellous, and they move at everyone's walking pace. Make sure you or one of yours rides on it, not the funeral director.

Find one near you: type 'horse-drawn hearse' + your county into your search engine.

Motorcycle hearses

There are *motorcycle hearses*. Best known and utterly reliable is Motorcycle Funerals run by the Revd Paul Sinclair, the Faster Pastor, a huge character and a national treasure in his own right. 'Why', he asks, 'should those who love bikes be last seen in an automobile?' Quite so, Paul.

* Motorcycle Funerals – motorcyclefunerals.com. Ring: 01530 834616. Based in Leicestershire, operates UK-wide.

There are some hearse trailers out there pulled by trikes.

* Black Hawk Hearse – blackhawkhearse.co.uk.

Bicycle hearse

The Revd Paul also has a bicycle hearse. Ring for details.

Vintage lorry hearse

There is a *vintage lorry hearse* owned and driven by the splendid David Hall. He and his 1950 Leyland Beaver will drive anywhere. David has a gift for creating a display on the lorry's flat bed which reflects the life of the person who has died. Top chap.

* Vintagelorryfunerals.co.uk. Ring: 01225 865346.

4 × 4 hearse

For countryfolk, explorers and other aficionados of the all-terrain vehicle, Alpha 4 × 4 Funerals offer a silver Land Rover hearse and matching Zambesi 'limousine'.

* Alpha 4 × 4 Funerals: 4x4funerals.co.uk. Ring: 01234 720936. Based in Bedford.

VW hearse

For lovers of the VW camper van, Volkswagen Funerals offer a white VW Type 26 Bay hearse plus fleet of three white stretch Beetles. Alternatively, you can have the 1963 split-screen 21-window Samba. Based in Staffordshire.

- Volkswagen Funerals: volkswagenfunerals.co.uk. Ring: 01827 709067 or 01827 709045. Based in Staffordshire. Lovely people.

Thanks, we'll do it ourselves

If you would like to take your dead person on their final ride yourself, there is nothing to stop you from using or hiring your own preferred vehicle and taking them in that. Drive down to the undertaker's, load up and off you go. This way, you can go by any route you want and spend all the time you want – so long as you get to the church or crematorium on time. Be sure to have enough people to carry the coffin. And be sure to secure the coffin in the vehicle. You don't want it hitting the back of your head when you brake.

41

Marking the spot – memorials

So many ways to commemorate a life . . .

> Do not stand at my grave and weep;
> I am not there . . . (Mary Frye)

It is interesting to note that the instruction given in these, the opening words of arguably Britain's favourite funeral poem, are so often disobeyed.

This guide is no place to get psychological and try to analyse why we feel compelled to mark the spot where a loved one lies or was happy – or was killed, even, for roadside memorials for victims of traffic accidents or murder are a recent but well-established phenomenon.

Most people, whether religious or atheist, agree that, wherever their dead person is now, he or she is not there, not at the spot that they memorialize. Yet they do it all the same, and spend time at that spot, and tend it.

So, what purpose does a memorial serve?

Dr Johnson once asserted that 'grief is a species of idleness'. If he is right, then one remedy for grief is activity – busyness. A memorial certainly offers opportunities for therapeutic activity. It gives mourners

- somewhere to go;
- something to do.

If there's anything in Dr Johnson's theory, it is the physical rituals and observances associated with journeying to and tending a memorial and/or a grave which are emotionally nourishing. These rituals and observances enable you to

- do something *about* how you feel;
- do something *for* the person who has died;
- show the rest of the world that you care.

A memorial is physical evidence that someone once had a physical existence here on Earth. It proclaims that fact enduringly. The more eyecatching the memorial, the more loudly and publicly it proclaims it. It keeps that person in mind, perpetuates their memory. It remains an enduring point of contact with them, a place where you can go and talk to them. A memorial can be a bunch of flowers, a headstone, an obelisk, a shrine, a tree, a cairn. It can be anything, just so long as it is something.

You are not confined to just one memorial, either. You can both mark the spot and also keep the memory alive at another location or in other ways, privately or publicly. So a memorial can also be a folly, a charitable trust, a web page, a campaign, a horse-race, a half-marathon or a drop-in centre.

It is a matter for your individuality and wallet.

Why are so many cemeteries so tumbledown?

Conventional cemeteries cater for a spiritual and emotional need to commemorate someone for ever.

But the bleak truth is that families simply can't keep it up, all that remembering and grave tending. A visit to any cemetery will tell you that, after around ten years, very few visit a grave regularly any more. Graves of children are an exception. Parents will often visit until they die. But do you visit the graves of your grandparents? Your great-grandparents? Go to any big Victorian cemetery, survey the neglect and see how memorials of great size and magnificence have tumbled as they have succumbed to neglect. Marvel if you like at the absurdity of the expectation that future generations should maintain their monuments for ever. Vanity of vanities!

Britain's cemeteries are full of numberless unremembered graves and tottering monuments. They are testimony to the gradual obliteration of the unforgettable, to early-onset amnesia, to the futility of egoism.

If you plan to erect a headstone on a grave, it is worth bearing this in mind.

Restrictions on marking the spot

When a person is buried in a traditional burial ground, their plot is a sizeable space, a little piece of sovereign territory. It seems wholly right to mark the plot with a memorial. You can of course do just that in a traditional burial ground – a churchyard or a council-owned cemetery. In fact, it would look neglectful if you didn't.

But there are circumstances where it may be difficult, impossible or, you may think, pointless to mark the spot where the ashes or the body of someone who has died have been laid.

Natural burial grounds

A natural burial ground will restrict or even deny you any right to mark the spot and tend the grave (see Chapter 6).

If you bury someone in a natural burial ground you will have somewhere to go, but, in the truly green ones, nothing to do.

Scattered or buried ashes

Depending on where you scatter or bury ashes, marking the spot may be difficult. If you bury them in a cemetery, no problem, but if you scatter them in the garden of remembrance you will not be able to mark the spot.

If you scatter or bury them out in the country somewhere on land that does not belong to you, your scope for creating a physical memorial is virtually nil. Find out more about scattering ashes in Chapter 42.

When no one can visit

If no one can ever visit the spot because they all live too far away, there is, perhaps, little point in marking it. Any memorial you put up is soon going to get neglected.

What's more, a memorial arguably loses its point if no one ever goes there – but you may see it differently.

Can you put up a memorial which doesn't mark the spot?

If you feel a strong need to erect a memorial, even if it cannot mark the exact spot, you can of course do that and perhaps derive great solace from it. One or other of the following options may, you feel, be more satisfying than erecting a headstone at the grave.

A garden memorial

Create a memorial in your garden. Your options are boundless. You can commission a piece of sculpture and have it inscribed. You can dig a special flower bed or vegetable plot. You can plant a tree, make a shrine, instal a bench, create a herb garden, build a cairn.

If you're a fan of *New Tricks* you'll be familiar with James Bolan's character, Jack Halford, whose wife's ashes are buried in his lawn, surrounded by lights. He talks to her every evening. Perhaps you wouldn't want a memorial quite so bright – but you get the idea.

The great thing about a memorial in the garden is that it is physically close. An incidental benefit is that it will enhance your garden. This is probably why most people spend more money on a garden memorial than they would on a headstone in a burial ground.

If you're likely to move house at any time, choose a memorial you can take with you.

- Sarah Walton, potter: www.sarahwalton.co.uk.
- See under 'A bespoke headstone' below.

An online memorial

You can create a memorial in cyberspace. Members of the Facebook generation will have no difficulty getting their heads around this. If you find difficulty with the concept, consider this: only a memorial website can bring together a community of grieving people who are geographically scattered. It will give everyone somewhere to go and something to do any time they want, day or night.

An online memorial enables you to post memories, music and photos. It enables others to post their thoughts and memories. You can listen to favourite music while you watch a slideshow of photos. You can invite donations to charity in memory of the person who has died.

It is the greenest memorial available.

Choosing a dependable host site for your website is fraught with difficulty. First, many such sites have already foundered with all memories on board, so you'll need to find a host site which isn't going to go broke or stop upgrading. Second, a good many web developers have identified online memorial hosting as a moneyspinner, so there's a danger of being exploited. Third, a memorial site is potentially fertile ground for identity thieves, especially those sites which let anyone wander into anyone's memorial. You need to be sure that any site you like the look of has robust authentication and privacy controls, and is effectively monitored.

Three factors determine the quality of an online memorial site:

- ethics – including privacy safeguards;
- functionality – how does it drive? How fast does it go? Is it well equipped? Does it look good?
- a firm financial foundation.

Type 'online memorial' into your search engine to find out what's out there.

There are two market leaders, GoneTooSoon and MuchLoved. Of the two, Gone-TooSoon has an ethically questionable track record and has failed to respond to probing questions put to it by this guide.

Accordingly, we only recommend one memorial site, and we do so without reservation. It fulfils all the criteria.

- MuchLoved: www.muchloved.com. It is a registered charity, it is free and it is a signatory of the Online Memorial Code of Ethics: thememorialcode.org. In terms of functionality it outstrips its competitors.

Conventional ways of marking the spot

The conventional memorial is a headstone for a grave or, in the case of ashes buried or scattered in a cemetery, a tablet or plaque, a rose bush or a bench, whether marking the spot or situated nearby.

An off-the-peg headstone

Very few headstones are made from indigenous stone. Imported stone is, amazingly, cheaper to quarry and transport. Chinese granite is the favourite, in black, grey, blue or red. Next is marble. In any cemetery, headstones in these materials are the overwhelming favourites. Some people don't think they fit in; others think they are very nice. What's more, they do not weather and granite is very easily wiped clean. Marble turns black.

You can buy a headstone off the peg in a choice of shapes for around £1,000 inclusive of an inscription of your choice plus installation. Your funeral director, if you use one, will either be able to handle all this for you, or put you in touch with a monumental mason.

Very little craftsmanship goes into creating a headstone or plaque like this. That's how they keep the cost down. The inscription is not carved, it is grit-blasted, as is any decoration you choose. Some people think headstones like this are very samey; others think they are just the job.

If you want something a little out of the ordinary, or an inscription which might shock, you should check first with cemetery management. Council-run cemeteries will try to be broadminded, but they have all sorts of restrictions designed to protect the ambience of the cemetery. Church-owned burial grounds will be much, much harder to satisfy in matters of choice and shape of stone and inscription.

You can add a photo-plaque to the headstone, but not in a Church of England burial ground.

Your monumental mason will advise you about all your options, as well as all the rules and regulations. Find a more or less competent monumental mason here:

*   The National Association of Memorial Masons – namm.org.uk. Ring: 01788 542264.

A bespoke headstone

If you would like a bespoke headstone there are stone carvers and lettercutters who will make you one and do exactly as you ask. Such a headstone will be much more expensive and a thousand times more beautiful and personal. Average cost: £3,000. Sky's the limit, of course.

*   Memorials by Artists: memorialsbyartists.co.uk. Ring 01728 688934. Essentially an agency for the best carvers and lettercutters in the UK. They publish an illustrated guide to commissioning a memorial and a separate guide to commissioning a memorial for someone under the age of 30.

*   Ieuan Rees, lettercutter: www.ieuanreeslettering.co.uk. Ring 01269 593471. Based in Wales.

• Stone Carving and Memorials: stonecarving.co.uk. Ring: 01547 528793. Will and Lottie O'Leary. Based in Powys.

Other memorials in a cemetery

Even natural burial grounds which forbid all forms of memorialization are beginning to give in to demand and allow the names of their occupants to be recorded where all can see. People's impulse to have this public record is very strong.

Your local cemetery or crematorium will enable you to buy a plaque for a fixed term, renewable, located on a wall or installation for £100–£500. You may be able to buy a memorial rose bush, a bench or a flagstone in a paved footpath. You will be able to have the name of the person who has died inscribed in a book of remembrance, perhaps an electronic one.

• Find out what your options are: ask your funeral director or contact your local cemetery or crematorium.

Grave tenders

If, for whatever reason, you are going to find it difficult to tend a grave or memorial, there is a growing army of grave tenders out there who will do it for you, and send you a photo to prove they did.

• Type 'grave-tending' + your area into your search engine.

42

What to do with the ashes?

Yes, you can scatter them.

But what else can you do with them?

There's a finality about burial. It's all over, you think, as the coffin descends.

It is.

Cremation gives you no such conclusion. You get a version of the body back – if you want it. Cremated remains, or ashes, as most people call them, are mostly pulverized bone. They weigh around as much as the dead person did when they were born, so there's a nice symmetry there.

If you decided not to have a funeral for the body but opted for direct cremation in order to prepare the body for a funeral, now's your chance to have one pretty much anywhere you like.

If you did have a funeral for the body and it was an unsatisfactory occasion, here's a second chance to get it right.

What to do with them?

You can bury ashes in your local cemetery or in a natural burial ground. You can scatter them. You can divide them up among members of the family. You can get the crematorium to scatter them. You can do hundreds of things with them.

Many people only start to think creatively after they've brought the ashes home – sometimes long after. During this time the ashes may sit on the mantelpiece, the wardrobe, the boot of the car – dry, warm and safe. Of course, they're more than just ashes and they deserve a fitting destination. This is a very personal thing, so does it matter in the least what other people think? Rolling Stone Keith Richards snorted some of his father's ashes. Patsy Kensit slept beside her mother's for years. A distinguished pathologist, Derek Roskell, wants his ashes be scattered over Tony Blair. Denise Moon took the ashes of her late partner to court to prove that she was not evading council tax. Gene Roddenberry, creator of *Star Wars*, was shot into space. We make sense of things in our own way. That way may not seem logical to other people, but logic may well have a negligible part to play in the matter of farewelling our dead or, indeed, of making sense of anything.

A favourite way with ashes is to scatter them at a spot which the dead person loved. But there are drawbacks you ought to consider.

First, if this is a popular beauty spot, you may feel inhibited by the proximity of other people. You won't have a good experience if you wait anxiously till no one's looking and then do it surreptitiously. So many people do this at Jane Austen's cottage that hurriedly tipped remains have become an unsightly nuisance.

Second, if the beauty spot you favour is a mountain top or an upland location, the phosphate in the ashes will upset the ecology. It's a poor way to commemorate someone, to turn them into a bio-hazard. This is why football grounds will not let you scatter ashes on the pitch.

Make a ceremony of it. Choose a place where you can hold that openly and joyously and safely.

Here are some other things you can do with ashes:

- Keep them in an urn. There's a vast range out there, with new products coming onto the market all the time. Your funeral director may not be aware of all of them. Use your search engine.

- Mix them with clay or concrete and make something.

- Mix some with paint and paint something – or commission an artist.

- Fire them out of shotgun cartridges.

- Scatter them from a hot air balloon or a light aircraft.

- Scatter them at sea.

- Have them turned into a diamond. Go to phoenix-diamonds.com.

- Have them mixed with glass and made into an ornament or pendant. Go to ashesintoglass.co.uk.

- Keep some in a locket, a ring or a pendant. Go to urns-coffins-caskets.co.uk.

- Have them made into a firework display. Go to heavensabovefireworks.com.

- Fire them into space. Go to heavensabovefireworks.com.

Your range of choices is as wide as your imagination.

43

What does dying feel like?

Most of us live longer these days than ever before. There is an assumption that this is a good thing, but, given the consequences, this is debatable. Never before has there been such an intense debate around the subject of euthanasia and assisted suicide.

Longer life often comes at a cost. To opt for a puritanical regime of healthy lifestyle choices supported by superb medical care may simply enable your virtuous body to outlive your blameless brain by years of bewildered incontinence. Are we living longer or merely lingering longer? What price prolonged decrepitude? Around half of all complaints against the National Health Service relate to the care of the dying.

For sure, it's never taken so long to die once we've contracted the illness that will do us in. And though, in good times, life is precious to us and death a catastrophe, there have probably never been so many alive who earnestly desire to depart in peace, or whose death is earnestly desired by those who love them, as a merciful release.

There are those who fear death and those who say they don't. A quite separate matter is dying, and we are all justified in fearing that. We know that our end will likely be a difficult rearguard action protracted by the helpful, often urgent, intervention of brilliant medics. If you have spent time by the bed of a dying person, you know that keenly.

And in a dark place at the back of your mind, you wonder sometimes how you will feel as you tilt from this world into the void or wherever.

The good news is that dying, for most, feels good. And this news comes not from wishful speculators but from men and women of science for whom evidence and verifiability are the only tests of truth. In his book *The Art of Dying*, Peter Fenwick, a neuropsychiatrist and neurophysiologist, together with his wife, Elizabeth, collate and assess research into the experiences of dying people.

The Fenwicks talk about ELEs – end-of-life experiences – when some dying people become aware of the friendly presence of dead people, often family members, who have come for them to guide them on their journey. Here's a typical account:

> Suddenly my Gran sat up in bed and smiled. She said, 'I'm going now, and here's Dad and George come to meet me.' She then died, still with this big smile on her face.

And here's another:

> My father was at [his father's] bedside, deeply distressed, but my grandfather said to my father, 'Don't worry, Leslie, I am all right, I can see

and hear the most beautiful things and you must not worry.' And he quietly died, lucid to the end.

These experiences are invariably deeply moving and spiritually meaningful for those who witness them, and they invariably dissolve their fear of death.

The Fenwicks conclude that 'a mechanistic view of brain function is inadequate to explain these transcendent experiences'. They refute any claim that they are drug-induced experiences in dying people on the grounds that drugs give rise to altogether more psychedelic hallucinations.

The Fenwicks talk about the experiences of people miles away from a dying person who become aware of their death at the precise time it happens.

They talk about how sometimes the living have a continuing sense of the presence of a dead person.

They're especially interesting about NDEs – near-death experiences – especially those they term TDEs – temporary death experiences. Some survivors of cardiac arrest experience the classic near-death experience *even though they are technically dead*. The Fenwicks conclude: 'From the point of view of science, TDEs cannot occur during unconsciousness, and yet there is some tantalizing evidence that this is just when they do seem to occur.'

They propose that consciousness may not be limited to the brain, and that, given the lovely time people have dying, 'a greater understanding of what happens when we die would lead to a removal of our fear of death and open up the possibility of a new beginning, the start of a new journey'.

The inference here, of course, is that there must be some sort of afterlife.

Read the book:

- *The Art of Dying* by Peter and Elizabeth Fenwick, published by Continuum.

Where do we go when we die?

It is not the place of this guide to stray outside verifiable reality and speculate on the journey that dead people tread, nor their destination. But if you want to find out more about scientific attempts to identify the soul, investigate reincarnation, spirit mediums and other paranormal, afterlife phenomena, American writer Mary Roach has written a sceptical, readable survey:

- *Six Feet Over* by Mary Roach, published by Canongate.

44

Planning your own death and funeral

Making plans for your dying and your funeral is a chore easily postponed.

But as the years go by and increasing physical decrepitude makes it clear that you are not, after all, going to be the first person in history somehow to duck under the radar of the Grim Reaper, it feels more and more acceptable, even desirable, to make plans. Decrepitude is nature's way of reconciling us with the inevitable. Dementia may or may not be nature's way of taking our mind off it.

Whatever your state of decrepitude, remember this: the customary warning signs of impending death do not always apply. Pathologists will tell you that they spend their lives delving into the interiors of people who thought they'd be going home that very day, as every day.

Death often pre-dates decrepitude. It is only an embolism away.

If you're going to sit down and plan your funeral, it makes sense, at the same time, to make plans for the process which leads up to it: your dying.

Die prepared

Dying for most of us is going to be not a sudden event but a lengthy process. One of the dubious benefits of modern medicine is that it has greatly extended that process. The job of doctors is to prolong life, and they can easily, understandably, confuse this with prolonging the act of dying. Instead of letting us be borne out gently on the tide, they may instead launch a series of desperate, intrusive rearguard actions to stave off the inevitable.

You can prevent this – up to a point.

Your end-of-life plan needs to deal in detail with the following:

1. The disposal of your money and your things plus final instructions and directions to those who will have to settle your affairs when you're dead. This is often called putting your affairs in order.

2. How you are looked after in your last days.

3. Who will speak and act for you if you can no longer do so for yourself.

4. Where you die.

5. The way you die.

6. Whether or not your organs are recycled.

7. How your dead body will be cared for or to whom it will be donated.

8. How your dead body will be disposed of (burial or cremation).

9. Who you would like to be told that you are dead.

10. Your funeral ceremony.

11. The party afterwards.

A plan like this spans several separate professional domains, each of which is colonized by its own specialists – solicitors, will writers, financial advisers, medics, undertakers, celebrants and caterers – all of whom mind their own business.

The only person who can join them all up is you.

When death seems to be the hardest word . . .

In communities where cultural or religious traditions are strong, people don't worry about their funeral. They know that, when the time comes, those closest to them will know what to do; custom and duty will see to it that things are done properly. This eliminates choice, but it also eliminates faffing.

In communities where traditions have been left behind, dying people have no such assurance. When death happens, unless they have been told, those closest to them won't necessarily have a clue what to do.

If those closest to you do not know how you want to be cared for as you lie dying, and, afterwards, how you would like your dead body to be cared for and disposed of, you will need to tell them.

And your problem may well be that, when you try to do so, you will walk into a storm of protest. We live in death-denying times.

Where death is not reckoned to be the boarding pass to eternal life, talk of it is unwelcome. While people of much faith stride confidently into that good night, those of little faith or none at all tend to put their hands over their eyes and reveal a morass of squirming superstitions. Talking about death is reckoned morbid; worse, it's likely to bring it on.

One of the reasons why people don't talk about death is that no one will listen.

We need to talk

However reluctant they are, you will need to try to talk to those closest to you about how you would like to make your exit because, if you want them to be your advocates (see below), you'll need their active involvement. Tell them that if they truly love you, they will listen. Tell them that, when you can no longer speak for yourself, you will urgently need them to be there to speak and act for you.

In the face of any initial reluctance, you need to be persuasive because you need their agreement. You need to negotiate face to face in order to reach an understanding. You need to listen and, perhaps, give ground.

You should resist the temptation to issue instructions or resort to emotional blackmail. Agreements extorted under duress may not be honoured – and you will be in no position to protest.

Your goal is to engage willing collaboration.

Talking about your death is likely to upset those you talk to. It may well upset you, too. But when you have done it, you are all likely to feel that sense of relief which comes with having dealt with an unspoken dread.

When the time comes, those closest to you will be informed, prepared and empowered. They will be able to be useful, and they'll like that.

If you can't find anyone who will listen, you have no alternative but to write down what you want and hope that someone will act on it.

You will be able to transmit your care wishes through a living will, and these will be respected.

You will probably be able to exert a degree of influence over your funeral, especially if you buy a pre-paid funeral plan, of which more later.

What is a good death?

There is a good deal of talk nowadays about dying a good death. This is nothing new: people have always wanted to die well, on their own terms, in their own homes, courageously, with no regrets, with all their affairs in order, surrounded by their loved ones with whom they are at peace. Sad, yes, but serene, especially if the dying person is old, loved and has led a good and fulfilled life.

There are two sides to a good death: what's going to be best for you and what is going to be best for those closest to you. Of the two, most dying people worry more about the impact of their death on others and understandably want it to cause them as little grief as possible.

A good death gives you time. Maxine Edginton died of cancer in 2006. Before she died, she wrote a song with Billy Bragg, entitled 'We Laughed', dedicated to her sixteen-year-old daughter. Hear it on YouTube. Speaking on Radio 2's *Jeremy Vine Show*, Maxine spoke of her thoughts when she was told her illness was terminal:

> I just realized that dying was not actually about me, it was about those around me; it was about their feelings, it was about their comfort, it was about their coping, their knowing that I loved them, and it was leaving nothing unsaid.

Different people will have different opinions about what constitutes a good death. For most, a good death will combine all or most of the following elements:

- All the administration sorted – will, living will, funeral wishes.

- Nothing left unpaid, and dependants provided for.

- A lead-in time – a week at the least.

- The place of your choosing (home for most people).

- Symptoms controlled, especially pain and nausea.

- A life lived well – no regrets.

- A long life.

- Acceptance.

- No unresolved relationship issues – no guilt, no feuds.

- Nothing left unsaid – last words and farewells for everyone.

- Spiritual support.

What is a bad death?

A bad death, like a good death, is a matter of perception.

Any sort of sudden, unexpected death is, most people would reckon, a bad death – particularly for those who are left. Worse still if the dead person had not left their affairs in order. Worst of all if the cause of death was suicide, murder or a drugs overdose.

A bad death is one where a person dies emotionally unprepared in a state of terror or rage or guilt.

A bad death may be a difficult death, when a person dies after a very long, uncomfortable illness. Such a death is often described as a merciful release.

If, though, that person had refused medication to control their symptoms on the grounds that they wanted to remain alert, then their suffering may be reckoned heroic and their death both a good death and a merciful release.

A bad death is one when a person feels they have lost their dignity. Dignity means different things to different people. Some people retain a sense of dignity in even the most 'undignified' of circumstances; others arrive at a stage of dependency when their dignity is gone, their situation intolerable and their death a desirable release.

Loss of dignity may be a consequence of illness or it may be the consequence of the actions of medics trying fruitlessly to keep you alive. To die full of tubes with a doctor pounding your chest in a pointless effort to revive you could be described as both a bad way to go and a merciful release. Because so many people die under medical supervision, there's a good chance that your own death will contain elements of a bad and a good death.

It's all a matter of perception.

It is not only doctors who can deny us dignity at the end. Dementia can do that, and it's doing it to more and more of us. A consequence of healthy living and improved medical science has been our ability to add years to the wrong end of our lives; for our nutrient-rich bodies to continue functioning incontinently long after our brain has decayed.

You can't help being the victim of rapid or sudden death, but you can mitigate its effects by having left your affairs in order and written letters to your loved ones to be opened when you die.

Find out more

The BBC publishes an excellent booklet, *Planning a Good Death*, downloadable as a PDF file. For this and other good information, go to: bbc.co.uk/health/tv_and_radio/how_to_have_a_good_death.

Five Wishes – agingwithdignity.org.

The American charity Aging With Dignity publishes a booklet called *Five Wishes*, available as a read-only PDF file on their website. Although it is designed in accordance with US law, it is full of things that you will want to think about in making your end-of-life plan.

Assisted suicide and self-deliverance

There are degenerative conditions which cause us to linger long after we might wish we could have gone. Motor neurone disease is one. Some afflicted people assert their right to die on their own terms either by killing themselves or by finding someone to help them. It's illegal to assist a suicide in the UK, but less so in parts of Europe. British people go to Switzerland to do away with themselves, and you have doubtless read about them.

Find out more

- Dignity in Dying: dignityindying.org.uk. Their mission: to secure the right for everyone to be able to die with dignity at the end of their life.

- Exit: euthanasia.cc. Similar in aims to Dignity in Dying. Based in Scotland. Lots of articles for and against euthanasia.

- Dignitas: dignitas.ch. The Swiss organization which offers self-deliverance.

Your end-of-life plan 1: Put your affairs in order

You probably feel that it is a duty to make sure that your money and your possessions go to those whom you want to have them. You know, especially if you have dependants, that, if you haven't yet done so, you ought to make a will. There's plenty of advice out there about how to do that, and there's no time like the present: just get on with it. See a solicitor or a will writer – or buy one of those forms they sell in the Post Office. You may want to consult a financial adviser, too.

You probably think that it is thoughtful to spare your nearest and dearest an orgy of sorting when you're gone. An additional excellent way of putting your affairs in order is to fill in the information sheet 'Instructions for my next-of-kin and executors upon my death', which you can download from the Age Concern website (ageconcern.org. uk). On this well-designed form you can record essential personal information and list all the people you want to be told of your death. You can also record your outline funeral wishes here, too, if you like. Make sure someone knows where they can find it.

You may like to fill a memory box with letters, photos and other mementos of yourself.

Perhaps you would like to record and leave behind, in some way, your life story, or some stories from your life, or your thoughts about life. The Charity Rosetta Life works with people who are dying and helps them to express whatever it is they want to say, in the way they want to say it. Their website – www.rosettalife.org – has an online gallery of people's life stories. You may find them inspiring.

You may think it helpful, if there's likely to be any haggling, to put discreet stickers on some of your things, assigning them to individuals.

If you have pets, you need to make provision for them. If you have no one to take them on, the RSPCA's 'Home For Life' service will look after and, if possible, rehome them. You can download a registration form from their website (rspca.org.uk), or you can get them to send you one – phone 0300 1234 999. The form includes the wording you will need for your will. Be aware that the RSPCA has a reputation for making it increasingly difficult for people to adopt animals. They say they will not put a pet down at the end of a fixed period. An even more dependable bet for your dog may, you feel, be the Dogs Trust (dogstrust.org.uk), who undertake never, ever, to put an animal down. Phone them: 020 7837 0006.

Last letters

Should you happen to die suddenly – in, say, a car crash – you will miss the chance to utter any last words. It is therefore worth thinking about writing letters to those closest to you now, and enclosing them with your will.

Not an easy thing to do when you are in the best of health. Is this a good idea for you? Try visualizing the scene at home in the event of your sudden death, then follow your impulse.

Your end-of-life plan 2: Find an advocate

If you lose touch with what's going on in this world during your final illness – there's a good chance you will – you will need one or more collaborative people to be your advocates, to deal with each set of professional specialists in turn and see that your wishes are carried out. Remember: for as long as you are alive, you have all sorts of legal rights which ensure that your wishes will be respected.

Anyone can be your advocate – a family member or an old friend. It is potentially a time-consuming job, and it may well be a burdensome responsibility. Be aware of this when you are asking someone to be your advocate.

Your end-of-life plan 3: Make a living will

If you want those treating you to know how you would like to be looked after when you can no longer speak for yourself, you can make what is often called a living will. There are two sorts of living will:

- an *advance statement*;
- an *advance directive to refuse treatment* (ADRT).

An advance statement

You can use an advance statement to state your wishes, values and preferences. If, in the course of your illness, you should lose your mental capacity or the power to communicate, an advance statement will help those treating you to decide how you would like them to act.

You may wish to draw up your advance statement in consultation with your doctor and have it included with your medical notes. It is not legally binding, but it will certainly be respected – and it will greatly help your advocate or advocates to represent you.

In your advance statement you may like to address the following:

- Preferences for your health care, especially pain relief. For example, do you want any pain to be completely relieved even if that makes you very sleepy?
- The names of those whom you wish to speak for you.
- Do you wish to be visited by a faith leader?
- Do you want to be told that you are dying?
- Who do you want to be told that you are dying?
- Where do you want to die (home, hospital, etc.)?
- Who do you want to be present while you die?

- Do you want to die alone?

- Do you want music playing or somebody reading?

An advance directive to refuse treatment – ADRT

An advance directive deals exclusively with your medical care and addresses, particularly, the lengths you want your doctors to go to keep you alive.

You cannot require medical people to do things they don't want, but you can stop them from doing things you don't want. So, you cannot ask your doctors to put you out of your suffering, but you can stop them from administering life-sustaining treatment such as cardiopulmonary resuscitation (CPR).

If you want to limit your treatment and allow your doctors to let you die, you will need to write an advance directive to refuse treatment, sometimes known by its initials as an ADRT. You will probably want to do this in consultation with your GP and your advocates.

An ADRT is legally binding. You can draw one up with your solicitor or you can do it yourself.

You can download a form for £25 from:

- Dignity in Dying: dignityindying.org.uk.

- Ring them on: 0870 777 7868.

You can buy, for just £5, forms outlining your Death Plan, ADRT and Advance Funeral Wishes from the Natural Death Centre. Highly recommended.

- Order online: naturaldeath.org.uk.

- Ring them: 0871 288 2098.

Find out more about living wills

Age Concern – ageconcern.org.uk.

Age Concern publish superb, free information leaflets downloadable in PDF format about all aspects of end-of-life planning. They are informative, comprehensive and easy to understand. Note: some of the information in them may not apply if you live in Scotland or Northern Ireland. Your best bet is to consult ageconcernscotland.org.uk or ageconcernni.org. Neither website is half as helpful as its English counterpart.

- In England, click on the 'Information and advice' button at the top, then click on 'Factsheets'. Download the PDF FS7 (Factsheet 7), which will tell you about making a will. Then download FS22, all about powers of attorney. Lastly, download FS27, about funeral planning.

- Go back to 'Information and advice' and then go to 'Information guides'. Download 'Putting your affairs in order'.

- Go back to 'Information and advice' and then go to 'Information sheets'. Download IS5 about living wills and IS18: 'Instructions for my next-of-kin and executors upon my death'.

You can phone Age Concern:

- England: 0800 00 99 66.

- Scotland: 0845 833 0200.

- Northern Ireland: (028) 90 24 57 29.

Directgov – direct.gov.uk

Good down-to-earth advice plus a useful example of a living will. At the home page type 'living will' into the search box.

- Five Wishes – agingwithdignity.org

Your end-of-life plan 4: Award powers of attorney

Ordinary power of attorney

If you can no longer physically conduct your financial affairs, you may want to give an advocate *power of attorney* – often called *ordinary power of attorney*. He or she can then pay your bills and get money from your bank.

Ordinary power of attorney comes to an end if you lose control of your mind.

Lasting power of attorney

Should you lose your mental powers while you are ill, you may want to instruct your advocate or advocates to:

- represent your care wishes;

- conduct your financial affairs.

If so, you will want to give them *lasting power of attorney* (LPA). Lasting power of attorney has superseded enduring power of attorney (EPA), but EPAs are still valid.

There are two types of LPA:

- a personal welfare LPA;

- a property and affairs LPA.

In each case you must fill out an official form and register it with the Office of the Public Guardian (OPG) for a fee. The OPG will ensure that your instructions are followed.

Lasting power of attorney comes to an end when you die.

You can draw up powers of attorney with your solicitor or you can do it yourself. Lawpack – lawpack.co.uk – sell a Power of Attorney Kit, an information pack which comes with legal forms and an ADRT. Cost: £14.99. They also sell a Power of Attorney eKit minus ADRT downloadable online, cost: £9.99.

Find out more about powers of attorney

* Directgov – direct.gov.uk.

Good basic information on lasting powers of attorney (LPA), and you can download both a personal welfare and a property and affairs form. At the home page type 'Powers of attorney' into the search box.

• The Office of the Public Guardian (OPG) – publicguardian.gov.uk.

The OPG safeguards the interests of people who have made lasting powers of attorney and enduring powers of attorney. Go to 'Forms and booklets' on the home page (bottom left) and download everything you need to know about lasting power of attorney.

* Phone the OPG on: 0845 330 2900.

Your end-of-life plan 5: Recycle your body

You may wish to include in your end-of-life plan a request for your body, or for parts of your body, to be made use of after your death.

Be an organ or tissue donor

When you die you may, like an old car, have parts which other people can make use of. If you want to donate parts of your body, and you have joined the NHS Donor Register, those closest to you may be shocked if they didn't know, when the medics tell them, but they will not be able to overrule you. If, on the other hand, you don't want this to happen, they will be able to stop it from happening.

Often, organs and tissue are removed from people who have died but whose heart is still beating. This is because the person has died of a head injury, a stroke or a haemorrhage, and their brain is dead but their heart can be kept beating for as long it receives oxygen from a ventilator. In such a case, two doctors have to diagnose brainstem death first. They really do make absolutely sure that you are dead!

When they have taken the organs and tissue they can use, they switch you off and stitch you up neatly.

Find out more at the NHS website: uktransplant.org.uk, or phone them: 0845 60 60 400.

Note: if you do want to donate organs, don't rely on someone finding your donor card. Register with the NHS Organ Donor Register on the website above, or ring the NHS Organ Donor Line: 0845 60 60 400.

Give your body to medical science

Only you can donate your body to medical science. If you do, it will be called a cadaver and dissected over a period of up to five years – usually three – by medical students learning anatomy. Despite high-tech teaching aids like computer-generated 3D images, medical schools still want real-life bodies, and they are currently not getting enough.

We've all heard the stories about the japes that the students used to get up to with dead bodies, so: will your body be treated with respect? The answer is: nowadays, unquestionably, yes. And all your body parts will be kept together and cremated or buried as you wish at a ceremony which the students will go to. Says Shaun, a third-year student, 'It was a moving and humbling experience, going to say goodbye to my cadaver along with his family and a few close friends. Now, he was no longer a nameless body but someone with a life story who had lived and loved. My overwhelming feeling was of gratitude.'

You can donate your body, but it will only be used if it is in reasonable condition and if your next-of-kin agree, so you will need to make them aware and persuade them to agree. A post mortem, amputation, infectious disease or dementia will rule it out; so may dying outside medical school term time. You have to be over seventeen, and you will need to contact your nearest medical school for a consent form.

For further information, go to the Human Tissue Authority website: hta.gov.uk, or phone them: 020 7211 3400.

When they have finished with you, the medical school pays for the funeral.

Brain banks and in-house tissue banks

Brain banks store tissue for research into neurological disorders. If you have a neurological disease like Parkinson's or Alzheimer's, your brain can be very useful for research. It may also be possible to discover if there is a genetic element to your disease, and your family can be told about this.

Brain banks don't just need diseased brains, they need healthy ones, too, so that they can compare.

For further information, contact the Human Tissue Authority.

Your end-of-life plan 6: Your funeral

If you have read the previous chapters of this guide you will probably have begun to think about your role in planning your own funeral.

You will have thought about how you can balance your needs and wishes against the needs and wishes of the people closest to you. Above all, you will have considered to what extent they will wish to participate in arranging your funeral. You may already have discussed it with them.

You will have thought about how you want your body to be looked after before it is disposed of, and you will have thought about what sort of funeral ceremony you would like – if you would like any sort of ceremony at all. If you do, you may already have a clear idea about what shape you would like it to take: the music and the readings you would like – if any – and who you would like to talk about you – if anyone.

You will have thought about the 'do' afterwards.

You will have thought about whether or not you want a memorial service.

You will have thought about who is going to pay for your funeral, and how much.

You will have thought about the effect of your death on other people and whether, in its aftermath, they will be emotionally capable of arranging your funeral. You may have concluded that they won't be up to it, or you may take the view that they will know what to do when the time comes.

Different people decide differently according to their beliefs, values and personal circumstances. Only you can decide what to do for the best, and this guide cannot offer one-size-fits-all advice.

In order to help you reach the right decisions, both for you and for those who will be responsible for arranging your funeral, let's examine some of the concerns and anxieties that many people have, some of which you may share.

'I want to spare their feelings as much as possible'

It is natural to want to protect those whom you love from the emotional impact of your death. But, however great your desire to spare people's feelings, your death is going to bring them grief proportionate to their feelings for you. Their grief will be their expression of their love for you. You cannot legislate for the emotions of other people. They'll have to cope in the best way they can – it's a fact of death.

There is nothing you can do to diminish the impact of your death. The only way you can help is by not making matters worse.

Ways of making matters worse may include:

• Refusing to talk about your death, and how you feel about it, on the grounds that doing so will be upsetting. Mistake. The more others can see how reconciled you are, the more easily they will be able to reconcile themselves.

- Playing such a controlling part in planning your funeral that you deny others the opportunity to mourn and celebrate you in the way they need.

'I want to cause as little trouble as possible'

You may want to try to minimize the impact of your death by telling people that you want as little fuss as possible.

It may be helpful here to consider an analogy and think about what your funeral will have in common with your birthday. Unlikely as it may appear, there could be important and instructive similarities between these two very different-seeming events.

Your birthday party is an event created *by* other people *for* you.

When asked what you'd like for your birthday, you probably modestly protest that you don't want anyone to spend lots of money and put themselves out on your account. No fuss, please. And no expense.

After some arm-twisting, you probably helpfully hint at what presents you'd like, and what sort of celebration. Then you leave it to others, wait for the day and, hopefully, enjoy the ride.

The part you play on your birthday is mostly passive. You graciously, gratefully undergo what has been planned for you. Hopefully, it's a series of lovely surprises.

The part played by others is active. The more they think of you, the more they do, and the more fun it all is. You find out what other people think of you on your birthday. The celebration may cost them a great deal of money or very little. This is of little or no account compared with the amount of thought and hard work they put into it. But you will never hear anyone say, 'The only good birthday is a cheap one.'

It would be unthinkable for you to spare other people the hassle and expense of organizing your birthday by buying your own presents, arranging your own party and then inviting everyone along. It would be weird and even repulsive.

It would also miss the point. This is because there are two essential elements to a birthday celebration:

- the joy of receiving (yours);
- the joy of giving (theirs).

And unless these two essential elements are present, also, at your funeral, the event risks missing the point. Sure, you will be denied the first-hand joy of receiving, being dead, but those who know and love you will be able to experience this joy on your behalf. This is why one of the first things people say after a funeral, if it's any good, is, 'He/she would have loved that.'

A funeral is an event created *by* other people *for* you. If you deny others participation in planning the event, and the joy of giving you the send-off they think you deserve, you take away its most important element, the joy of giving. You deny those closest to you any role beyond that of passive bystanders.

So there is a very good case for simply letting them get on and do what they need to do with minimal input from you.

There are, of course, significant differences between a birthday and a funeral. For one thing, it is considered good manners to write a blank cheque for your funeral. This may sound like an important difference, but actually it may not be. Let's think about money next.

'I feel I ought to pay for my funeral'

You can't spare people's feelings when you die, but you can spare them the expense of your funeral. Most people make sure they leave enough money to cover all the expenses. They feel they ought. It is the customary thing to do.

There are all sorts of ways you can fund your funeral. If you are clever with money, there is, doubtless, nothing this guide can teach you about the best way of doing that. If you are not, here are three popular options:

- Put some money aside in a high-interest bank account.

- Buy an ISA.

- Buy a whole-life insurance policy.

You can also buy a pre-paid funeral plan, and we'll come to that.

'How much money should I set aside?'

The cost of dying, calculated on what people actually spend, presently stands close to an average of £7,000. London is the most expensive place in which to die; the average cost there is £8,020.

Costs are predicted to rise by 38 per cent by 2012.

Where does the money go? Well, there's more to it than just funeral expenses:

1. Funeral – burial, £2,700, cremation £2,400.

2. Flowers – £229.

3. Death notice in the paper – £100+.

4. Catering – £341.

5. Headstone or other memorial – £100.

6. Administration of the estate – £2,507.

These are averages. You may well want to spend your money differently. But £7,000 or so looks like a useful sort of sum to squirrel away in a safe place.

'Surely a funeral plan is the best possible solution?'

A funeral plan – sometimes called a pre-need, pre-pay or pay-now-die-later plan – is a beguiling invention of the financial services industry acting in league with the undertakers. It enables you to buy tomorrow's funeral at today's price, and to die believing all your funeral arrangements to be in place and paid for.

When you buy a funeral plan you typically pay for:

- the undertaker's 'professional services';
- the care of your body;
- your coffin;
- a hearse plus any transport for mourners;
- doctors' fees;
- cremation or burial;
- priest or celebrant's fee;
- a proportion of the disbursements – but, note, a proportion only!

Most plans offer three or four funeral packages, all based on the so-called traditional funeral. Most also offer a bespoke option; personalization comes at a premium. You can pay in instalments or with a lump sum. Differences in price are determined principally by the poshness of the coffin and the number of limousines you want to convey mourners on the day of the funeral.

A funeral plan is mostly about merchandize, but you will be able to nominate who you want to conduct your funeral ceremony.

It looks like a financial bargain, especially with funeral expenses currently rising by around 10 per cent a year. How do they do it? Simply, they reckon they can grow your money faster than inflation – certainly faster than most readers of this guide can, definitely faster than a high-interest bank account. Is your money safe? Yes, absolutely. It's invested in a trust fund.

The funeral planners know how to play to your anxious desire to do the best for your family. They encourage you to suppose that the purchase of a plan is a considerate thing to do because it will spare your loved ones' feelings and their wallets.

Think carefully about the truth of what they say.

Golden Leaves stokes anxiety with this statement: 'Bereaved relatives have grief and anger to contend with. Adding the administrative burden of arranging the funeral to their confused and emotional state may lead to mistakes being made and unnecessary costs being incurred.' Is this, do you suppose, the state in which your loved ones will find themselves?

Golden Leaves goes on to make the claim that 'Planning and paying for your funeral in advance saves your family the anguish and grief of doing anything other than remembering you.' What on earth do you suppose they mean by that?

All undertakers market their funeral plans as aggressively as they decorously can. It's not primarily for your benefit, of course. These are cunning plans. The National Association of Funeral Directors recommends Perfect Choice plans to its membership as 'the perfect tool for your business . . . Designed FOR funeral directors BY working funeral directors'. Not much customer focus there.

For an undertaker, a funeral plan buys tomorrow's customer today. What is lending urgency to their sales pitch is that there's an ugly, bloody turf war going on out there in the funeral industry. The big conglomerates, Dignity Funerals and the Co-operative Group, are selling pre-need plans at a rate which threatens, come the near future, to throttle the life out of independent funeral directors.

Setting squabbling undertakers aside, it is true to say that, for some consumers, funeral plans represent a very good deal. If you can find an undertaker you like, you can arrange your funeral in advance and, by paying for it there and then, ensure that your funeral money is not subsequently swallowed up in nursing care fees. What's more, because you bought it when you were alive, it will not be subject to inheritance tax.

Experience shows that when someone buys a funeral plan, they spend less on their funeral than would their next-of-kin.

Remember, it will be your next-of-kin who will have to work with the appointed undertaker after your death, so there may be something to be said for involving them in the arrangement. It all depends on the closeness of your relationships, both emotional and geographic, with your family and/or the other important people in your life.

Be sure that this is what they would want. Be sure that, in buying a funeral plan, you will not deny others participation in planning your funeral and the joy of giving you the send-off they think you deserve. Be sure that they will not feel reduced to the status of passive bystanders.

Be aware, too, that your next-of-kin have no legal duty to honour your wishes. They can bury you even if you said you wanted to be cremated. They can buy extra services from the undertaker, and they can cancel any you have asked for which they don't like. They can, if they want, even cash in your funeral plan – though they will only get the sum you paid, not the matured sum, and they will lose from that an administration fee of around £155. You, too, can cash your plan in at any time – on the same terms.

There is very little difference between the terms offered by the funeral planners. The four distinctive players are:

- Dignity Funerals.

- The Co-operative Group.

- Golden Charter.

- Funeral Plans Online.

If you buy a Dignity or a Co-op plan, you will be tied to one of their funeral directors. If you buy an Age Concern plan you will most likely be tied to a Dignity funeral director. They say that this enables them to offer a guaranteed level of service. Golden Charter offers the plan favoured by the independents and the traditional family funeral directors, and lets you choose pretty much whoever you want. Funeral Plans Online is a sister company of Peace Funerals and it offers an ethical option: none of your money will be invested in arms manufacturers, cigarette makers, gamblers, human rights abusers or pornographers. What's more, your designated funeral director will be selected by Peace and, that being the case, you can rest assured that you will be buying a very good one.

Shop around. There are others.

Find out more

The Financial Services Authority (FSA), the government-appointed watchdog, explains funeral plans succinctly at http://www.moneymadeclear.fsa.gov.uk/products/funeral_plans.html.

Your end of life plan 7: Ceremony options

They say such nice things about people at their funerals that it makes me sad to realize that I'm going to miss mine by just a few days.' (Garrison Keillor)

In consdiering any desire you may have for your funeral to be as you want it, you will have considered the extent to which it is actually any of your business. It's being dead that makes all the difference. Is death a good time to butt out? It may be.

You can make your input to your funeral in the form of:

- instructions;

- wishes;

- abstention.

Instructions

You may take the view that, if you're paying for your funeral, you have every right to lay down exactly what is to happen. If you leave instructions, be aware that they may either be disobeyed or ignored; you have no human rights when you're dead. The only way to get people to do what you want is either to emotionally blackmail them or bribe them by making their obedience a condition of your will.

If, on the other hand, you are no longer particularly close to anyone, your instructions are likely to be indispensable.

Wishes

Your wishes are likely to be helpful, but you probably need to offer them in the clear understanding that they need not necessarily be adopted. It may be the case, for example, that you want a very simple ceremony, but those closest to you think you deserve something much more lavish. This isn't something they will be able to talk to you about; the best celebratory events often contain an element of surprise. You may want your funeral to be a cheerful occasion, but you cannot know whether or not this is how people will be feeling. You can't cheer people up by telling them to be cheery.

Abstention

If you wish to abstain from making any input to your funeral ceremony, it will be either because you are confident that you don't need to (they'll know what to do) or because you can't bear to think about it.

Find a celebrant

It can be difficult to find someone to talk to about your funeral if your family and friends either won't or are too far away. If you are in a hospice or a care home you may find that the care staff are neither trained nor inclined to talk about your funeral. Hospices are just beginning to address this missing link in end-of-life care, and high time, too.

The one person who will be able to talk to you honestly and unsentimentally without kidding you along is a faith leader or a celebrant.

There is much to be said for talking to a celebrant or a faith leader while you are still alive and, either on your own or with people close to you, create a draft or provisional funeral ceremony. This may bring you a great sense of peace that everything has been taken care of; that you can die with all your responsibilities discharged.

Find a caterer

When discussing your funeral ceremony, you may wish to talk also about the party afterwards. There is no correct, accepted term for an after-funeral party. It is sometimes called a wake, but really a wake is the time spent watching over the coffin before the funeral. Some people call it 'refreshments', some a reception, some a 'do'.

It is difficult for you to gauge what the mood will be at your funeral 'do'. The release of tension after the funeral, combined with the presence of family and old friends, many of whom may not have seen each other for some time, could well give rise to a party atmosphere – it often does. Alternatively, everyone may be so sunk in gloom that they will be inclined to eat and drink almost nothing.

Your wish may be to cheer everybody up and serve champagne. That may be appropriate – but not necessarily.

If you, your family and those closest to you can agree, there is everything to be said for making plans. Will it be a family affair? Will you need a venue? Will you need professional catering?

For some people, planning the after-funeral party can be a source of great solace and pleasure.

Now do it!

Now that you've thought about end-of-life planning, and what you need to do according to your own circumstances and the issues involved, you may like to make your own end-of-life plan.

Here, in summary, is a to-do list (to-die list, if you like). Tick the ones you are going to do something about.

End of life to-do list

- ☐ Will.
- ☐ Final instructions and directions.
- ☐ List of people to be informed that I am dead.
- ☐ Last letters to loved ones.
- ☐ Nominate an advocate/advocates.
- ☐ Research self-deliverance.
- ☐ Make an advance statement.
- ☐ Make an advance directive (ADRT) or living will.
- ☐ Assign powers of attorney.
- ☐ Register with the NHS Organ Donor Register and list organs to be harvested.
- ☐ Donate my body to medical science.
- ☐ Find a funeral director and buy a pre-need funeral plan.
- ☐ Arrange my funeral ceremony with a faith leader/celebrant.

☐ Locate a venue for my funeral/memorial service.

☐ Arrange the after-funeral/after memorial service refreshments.

My funeral wishes

When I am dead

☐ I want _____ to be in charge of the arrangements.

☐ I want to be buried/cremated.

☐ The place where I want the funeral to take place is:

_____.

Is it important to you that your funeral arrangements are environmentally friendly?

☐ Yes /No

My body

These are my wishes/instructions for the care of my dead body.

I want my body to be looked after at home/at the funeral parlour.

I want my body to be laid out and dressed by:

_____ _____.

I want my body to be dressed in:

_____.

I do/do not want my body embalmed.

I do/do not want my mouth to be closed by suture.

I do/do not want my eyes to be kept shut by eyecaps.

The coffin I want is _____.

I want these people, if they wish, to come and visit my body:

_____

_____

_____

_____

_____.

On the day of my funeral

I want people to send flowers/I want people not to send flowers but to make donations to this charity/these charities:

_____

_____.

I want my body to be conveyed to my funeral in a:

_____.

I want no one to attend/anyone who wants to attend/the following only to be invited to attend:

_____

_____

_____.

I would like my family and/or close friends to follow in undertaker's limousine/s/ private cars.

I would/would not like a walking procession to the venue if possible.

I want these people to carry my coffin:

_____

_____

_____

_____.

The ceremony

I want the *ceremony* to be:

☐ religious;

☐ part-religious;

☐ atheist.

I want the *tone* of my funeral ceremony to be:

☐ happy and celebratory;

☐ quiet and reflective;

☐ as it happens to be.

I want people to *wear*:

☐ formal clothes;

☐ clothes with this theme _____ ;

☐ whatever they want.

I want the ceremony to be *led* by:

☐ a minister of religion;

☐ a secular celebrant;

☐ a humanist celebrant;

☐ members of my family and/or my friends.

This is the *music* I want:

_____

_____

_____ .

These are the *songs/hymns* I want:

_____

_____ .

These are the *readings* and *poems* I want:

_____

_____

_____.

The *person/people* I want to talk about me (deliver my eulogy or tribute) is/are:

☐ The person who is leading the ceremony.

☐ _____.

☐ In addition/instead, I would like a multimedia account/celebration of my life.

I want the ceremony to be:

☐ webcast;

☐ photographed;

☐ filmed.

If I am cremated

If I am cremated, I want my ashes to be stored in:

☐ whatever container the crematorium customarily uses;

☐ an urn. *Specify what sort of urn* _____.

Subsequently, I want my ashes to be disposed of in the following way:

_____.

I would like the spot to be marked in the following way:

_____.

If I am buried

I want the following to help dig and/or fill in my grave:

_____

_____.

I want my grave to be marked in this way:

_____

_____.

The inscription I would like on my headstone is:

_____

_____

_____

_____.

When it's all over

I want everyone/invited guests to meet up again at this venue:

_____.

I would like the following food and drink to be laid on:

_____

_____

_____.

Any special features?

_____

_____.

Other thoughts, wishes or instructions about my funeral

_____

_____

_____

_____.

Memorial service

I want/do not want a memorial service to be held after my funeral.

The place where I want the funeral to take place is:

_____.

I want the memorial service to be:

☐ religious;

☐ part-religious;

☐ atheist.

I want the *tone* of the service to be:

☐ happy and celebratory;

☐ quiet and reflective;

☐ as it happens to be.

I want people to *wear*:

☐ formal clothes;

☐ clothes with this theme _____ ;

☐ whatever they want.

I want the ceremony to be *led* by:

☐ a minister of religion;

☐ a secular celebrant;

☐ a humanist celebrant;

☐ members of my family and/or my friends.

This is the *music* I want:

_____

_____

_____.

These are the *songs/hymns* I want

_____

_____.

These are the *readings* and *poems* I want:

_____

_____

_____.

The *person* or *people* I want to talk about me is/are:

_____

_____

_____.

In addition/instead, I would like a multimedia account/celebration of my life.

I want the ceremony to be:

☐   webcast;

☐   photographed;

☐   filmed.

Any other thoughts, wishes or instructions

_____

_____

_____

_____

_____

_____

_____.